First and Goal

First and Goal

The CFL and the Pursuit of Excellence

Tony Proudfoot
Introduction by Darren Flutie

A Fenn Publishing Company Ltd. / Madison Press Book

Fenn Publishing Company Ltd.

Bolton, Ontario, Canada

Distributed in Canada by H.B. Fenn and Company Ltd.

Bolton, Ontario, Canada

www.hbfenn.com

Produced by

Madison Press Books

1000 Yonge Street, Suite 200

Toronto, Ontario

Canada M4W 2K2

www.madisonpressbooks.com

Printed in China

by SNP Leefung Printers Limited

Library and Archives Canada Cataloguing in Publication

Proudfoot, Tony

First and goal : the CFL and the pursuit of excellence / Tony Proudfoot.

ISBN 1-55168-316-4

1. Canadian Football League — History.

2. Football players — Canada — Interviews.

3. Canadian football — History. I. Title.

GV948.P76 2006   796.335'64   C2006-901303-9

All 300-plus pounds of
Pierre Vercheval, clearing
a path downfield.

Contents

Introduction

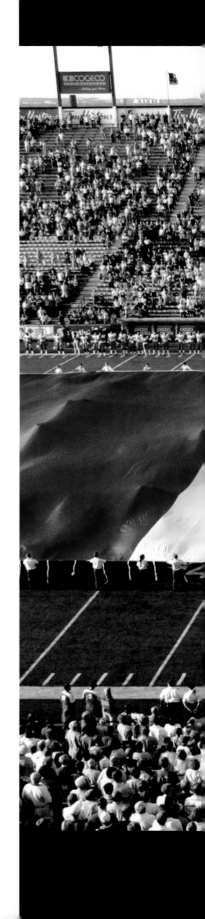

Arnold Palmer was once asked what made a golfer great. He responded with a now-legendary thought: "Golf is a game of inches. The most important are the six inches between your ears."

Comparing CFL football to golf is not something most football players, fans or analysts would risk, say, in a crowded Edmonton bar. But after reading Tony Proudfoot's insightful look at what makes the CFL's greatest tick, I think Palmer's quote is perfectly applicable to our game. Of course football players rely on speed, strength, size and athletic ability to withstand the intense physical punishment the game doles out. I have a career's worth of bumps and bruises that attest to that fact. However, as you'll see in the pages that follow, all of the CFL's finest – from my brother Doug at 5' 10" and 180 lbs to Brian Chiu at 6' 2" and 296 lbs – share two crucial characteristics: a profound understanding of the game and an unrelenting desire to be the best. It is this deep knowledge and passion, not only physical ability, that puts these players in a class of their own.

I knew early on in my football career that I would never be the fastest receiver in the game – or the strongest. But I worked hard, and over my career I watched thousands of hours of game film. I focused on myself, watching my routes, searching for clues that would allow me to take advantage of certain defensive schemes, certain defenders. And I learned how to get open in just about any situation. As a result, my quarterbacks through the years developed the confidence to throw the ball to me. It's thanks to those players, my hours of film work and my passion for the game that when I retired I was the CFL's all-time pass-reception leader.

I'm excited for CFL fans to discover this book. More than any other I've read, it gets inside the heads of the game's greatest players and reveals the real secrets of their dominance in this game we all love.

Thanks, Tony!

– Darren Flutie

I (23) enjoy the thrill of victory after the 1978 Eastern Final with my defensive back teammates (from left to right) Vernon Perry, Jim Burrows, Randy Rhino, Larry Uteck and Bruce Taylor.

Preface

I have wanted to write this book since I retired from playing the game twenty-some years ago. Canadian football has always intrigued me, because it is so mentally challenging and at the same time so elementally physical. I was able to survive in the league as a player not because I was the biggest, fastest or most athletic, but because I realized that being in the right position at the right time was the key to defensive performance. This game requires players to assimilate and apply a vast amount of knowledge to each and every play. I feel that most observers do not appreciate the level of sophistication and the depth of understanding that players routinely display throughout the game and, indeed, throughout their careers. I wanted to explore and challenge my convictions about football and find out what makes the best players tick. It is my objective in these pages to show what it takes to achieve greatness in the Canadian Football League and, in this way, celebrate both the players who have dominated the Canadian game and the game itself.

I interviewed forty-four players and coaches in the course of my research. Among them are some of the acknowledged giants of the game, Hall of Fame all-stars whose achievements are well known. Others are contemporary players who seem to me to exemplify the very best traits of players in their respective positions. Because greatness entails a degree of consistency, all the players I interviewed have compiled a record of achievement over at least six years in the professional game. No one-year wonders are featured here. The players whose voices are heard in these pages are the best of the best.

My approach has been, as far as possible, to let the coaches and players speak for themselves. They represent all positions of play, from offensive linemen to defensive backs. Even the often-overlooked – but essential – kickers are given their due. It is my hope that readers will come away from this book with a new appreciation for the skill, dedication and courage that the very best practitioners of Canadian professional football routinely exhibit on the field.

1

Rising Above It All

Football fans often refer to their local heroes as "great players," but how do current and former Canadian Football League coaches identify the greats among the many fine players that they have coached over the years? Eight CFL coaches interviewed for this book suggest that all great players possess the following three key characteristics: they perform consistently at a high level over a number of years; they possess a deep understanding of the game based on a willingness to learn; and they are mentally tough – that is, they exhibit confidence, courage and a willingness to take risks at crucial times.

ABOVE Chris Morris (60) and A.J. Gass (77) of the 2005 Edmonton Eskimos
enjoy the feeling that comes from winning that very last game of the year.

RIGHT In an emotional celebration in Montreal, running back Mike Pringle
is hoisted by his teammates during a ceremony to retire his number
after his thirteen glorious years as one of the league's most
singularly focused players ever.

Consistently High Performance

Marv Levy, for whom I had the good fortune to play, coached the Montreal Alouettes to several Grey Cup finals in the 1970s (winning the Grey Cup in 1974 and 1977) and then went on to a successful coaching career in the National Football League. He characterized great football players in the following way: "Obviously, basic athletic ability is a very important factor, but consistency over an extended period of time is truly the key – that is, a high level of performance over a span of at least six or seven years." The great player, he said, is "a guy that shows up for work every day, who is not looking for the glamorous aspect of the game so much – although he may love that part of his involvement – but he is in it because he truly enjoys the game, more than even the rewards."

Don Matthews, the Grey Cup–winning coach of the Montreal Alouettes in 2002 and the coach with the most wins in CFL history, also stresses the importance of consistently high performance. He notes that good players can have great seasons. They can even achieve big numbers and compile impressive statistics. But Matthews strongly believes that "great players continue to perform at a high level year after year."

Don Matthews plays the emotional card when he asks his team, "What time is it?" The answer? "Time to get busy!"

Statistics Don't Lie

Let's face it: the great players of the CFL perform. And the proof of their greatness can often be found in their statistics.

All-time Leading Passers

	Seasons	Passes	Completions	Yards
Damon Allen (1985–)	21	8,738	4,915	69,322
Danny McManus (1990–)	16	6,661	3,624	52,975
Ron Lancaster (1960–78)	19	6,233	3,384	50,535
Anthony Calvillo (1994–)	12	5,139	3,082	44,692

All-time Leading Receivers

	Seasons	Receptions	Yards	Average
Allen Pitts (1990–2000)	11	966	14,891	15.4
Darren Flutie (1991–2002)	12	972	14,359	14.8
Ray Elgard (1983–96)	14	830	13,198	15.9
Terry Vaughn (1995–)	11	948	13,051	14.3

All-time Leading Rushers

	Seasons	Carries	Yards	Average
Mike Pringle (1992–2004)	13	2,962	16,425	5.5
George Reed (1963–75)	13	3,243	16,116	5.0
Damon Allen (1985–)	21	1,738	11,702	6.7
Johnny Bright (1952–64)	13	1,969	10,909	5.5

All-time Leading Tacklers*

	Tackles
Willie Pless (1986–99)	1,241
Alondra Johnson (1989–2003)	1,084
Mike O'Shea (1993–2005)	968

* Recorded since 1987. With apologies to Marv Luster (1960–74), Wayne Harris (1961–72), Dan Kepley (1975–84) and possibly many other players from earlier eras.

All-time Leading Sackers*

	Sacks
Grover Covington (1981–91)	157
Elfrid Payton (1991–2004)	154
Bobby Jurasin (1986–98)	142

* Recorded since 1980. Apologies to older players, including Glen "Fuzzy" Weir (1972–84), Dave Fennell (1974–83), John Helton (1969–78), Jim Corrigall (1970–81) and possibly many others.

All-time Leading Interceptors

	Interceptions
Less Browne (1984–94)	87
Larry Highbaugh (1971–83)	66
Terry Irvin (1977–86)	62

Damon Allen (9) is the most striking example of an athlete who continues to play at a high level over an extended period of time. He has been compiling his staggering stats since 1985.

Ron Lancaster, currently senior director of football operations for the Hamilton Tiger-Cats and a lifelong participant in the CFL wars, shares the following story from his playing days in Saskatchewan that illustrates the ability of a great player to play consistently well under pressure. "We were playing Calgary and needed to win to finish in first place in the Western Conference. We were trailing by five points and were scrimmaging on our own five-yard line with only a few seconds left. I called for Rhett Dawson, a wide receiver, to run a deep seam route between the safeties. When the ball was snapped, the defensive rush was in my face sooner than I had expected, and I was forced to throw the ball sooner than I wanted to. I knew I was not going to be able to execute the deep seam pass I had called in the huddle, and I threw the ball deep to the sideline, not to the area where the receiver was supposed to be. I had a sense that Rhett recognized the predicament I was in by the defensive alignment, and he modified his route, knowing I wouldn't be able to throw a long pass down the middle of the field. As I unleashed the ball I was flattened, and it wasn't until I heard the crowd roar that I knew it was a long completion. Rhett and I smiled about that play for years to come."

"Great people are not afraid of risk or challenge, and they find a way of demanding more of themselves than others ever thought they had." – Mike Clemons

With nineteen years on the field (above, 23) and seventeen on the sidelines, Lancaster certainly qualifies as an authority on defining greatness.

The eyes tell it all: the fleet and intense Clemons using all his faculties to stay on top of his game. He currently holds the CFL record for all-purpose yards with an astounding 25,396.

"Greatness to me is not defined by a single game or even a series of games. Greatness has a longevity to it."

— Mike Clemons

Never one to shy away from a challenge, "Pinball" moved directly from player to head coach of the Toronto Argonauts. He conquered his new role with the same inimitable passion and enthusiasm with which he played.

Hugh Campbell, player, coach, general manager and current president and CEO of the Edmonton Eskimos, provided another example of the ability of great players to perform well in pressure situations. The player was defensive back Larry Highbaugh, a member of the Grey Cup-winning Edmonton Eskimos of the 1970s and 1980s. "We were playing in Regina," Campbell recalls, "and it was the last play. They needed a touchdown to win the game. They had about sixty yards to go. Larry, who was defending the designated receiver on the play, waited on the goal line for the Hail Mary pass to come down to the receiver on the five. He had the confidence to allow the receiver to catch the ball and then make the tackle five yards short of the goal line. We won, and afterwards I asked him what he was thinking. He told me that, because we were in Regina, he thought there would be less chance of an interference penalty if he did not contest the player

for the ball in the air, knowing all he had to do was concentrate on making the tackle." Only a great player would have the self-confidence to know he would make the big play flawlessly in a situation like this.

Mike "Pinball" Clemons, former CFL Most Outstanding Player and Grey Cup champion, was a great player before he became the 2004 Grey Cup-winning coach of the Toronto Argonauts. He agrees with Campbell's assessment and adds, "Great people are not afraid of risk or challenge, and they find a way of demanding more of themselves than others ever thought they had. More specifically related to football, I see great players as those who do those types of things, those things that cause us to turn around and take a second look, not once but on a consistent basis, not one year, but over the course of several years. Greatness to me is not defined by a single game or even a series of games. Greatness has longevity to it."

CLOCKWISE FROM TOP LEFT Marv Levy, Hugh Campbell, Gene Gaines and Wally Buono. Hundreds of years of combined football experience can't be wrong. Each member of this venerable group believes that players must fully develop their mental processes if they expect to become great.

A Willingness to Learn

While Levy, Matthews, Lancaster, Campbell and Clemons all emphasize the importance of consistency, Wally Buono, my teammate with the Alouettes of the 1970s and a highly successful CFL coach, stresses the importance of the understanding of the game that great players acquire. "The greatest players are able to process a tremendous amount of information when the pressure is the greatest. They do not crack under any form of pressure; in fact, they seem to thrive in that environment. One time I overheard our quarterback, Doug Flutie, explain to our offensive coordinator, John Hufnagel, how he was able to notice the releases of the slotbacks right off the line of scrimmage. Just from that bit of information early in the play sequence, he knew exactly when and where he was going to throw the ball. Remember, he is not even looking primarily at these players. It was just through the use of his peripheral vision that he could notice them." This level of confidence only comes when a player really knows the game and can appreciate how offensive and defensive schemes and individual movement patterns unfold. It is this deep knowledge, developed over years of practice and play, that allows great players to make good decisions at key times.

Hall of Famer Gene Gaines has forty-five years of experience as both a professional player and coach. He agrees that all great players are thinking players. "Absolutely, I don't know any who aren't. They are gifted with talent to a degree, but what makes them great is their motivation to go the extra mile, to be able to broaden their horizons. They are able to discern an important cue from way

It's a Canadian Game

Everyone knows that Canadian teams get just three downs — in contrast to the American four — to make their ten yards. The Canadian field is also bigger — twelve yards wider and ten yards longer than the American field. There are an extra ten yards in the end zone, too. This additional space gives the players more room in which to spread out and move.

In Canada, everyone except the five offensive linemen can move prior to the snap of the ball, and the defence must line up one yard from the line of scrimmage. These rules put a premium on agility rather than bulk for both the offensive and defensive teams. It's all about speed.

The National Football League allows only eleven men on the field. The CFL allows a twelfth man — who happens to be an eligible receiver. Finally, just forty players dress for a CFL game, compared to fifty in the NFL.

The effect of these differences is simple: Canadian football is a pass-oriented game, without the degree of specialization that characterizes the NFL. The Canadian game needs players who can run all day and perform a multitude of tasks. There are no 260-pound tight ends in the CFL, because players that big would never be able to run the fifty-or-so patterns per game that this league calls for. As well, many of the starting offensive and defensive players must perform on some or all of the kicking teams. Most CFL teams now employ five or six receiver sets on offence, requiring defences to match up with small, coverage-oriented defenders.

This means that players in the CFL have to be more versatile. They have to have a high level of cardiovascular endurance, a high strength-to-weight ratio, superior agility and better-than-average speed. CFL teams do not design their offences to grind away at the opposition, using strength and bulk to overwhelm them. Instead, the emphasis is on passing and the shrewd use of the kicking game.

out in left field. They are able to integrate that possibly small piece of information — maybe the angle of release of one of the receivers — and use that information to anticipate accurately what to do as a response. Paying attention to fine detail allows the better players to do a better job of anticipation. As time goes by, the pieces of each play, like in a puzzle, are easier to fit together, and as a consequence they can play with more confidence. They end up playing better without a doubt!"

Lancaster has seen thousands of football players in his time. "When you first come to this league," he says, "you are not necessarily going to be able to get everything right. First of all, you do not know enough about the demands of the CFL game, and secondly, you don't trust yourself to be able to pull it off, and so you don't have the confidence to take the risks that are required to be successful. You need to have the chance to develop, talk to other players and coaches, push yourself in practice to improve, and take risks in games...."

"I remember from my playing days with Saskatchewan that early on I knew that I needed to focus on personal improvement," Lancaster continues. "I learned a lot about how defensive cornerbacks play from my teammates Ray Odoms, Paul Williams and Steve Dennis. I would talk a lot with them, trying to understand how they played and what they reacted to in game situations. I competed with them in practice. I would ask them to try to intercept or break up every ball I would throw rather than let the receiver have it.... The coaches and the receivers didn't like having the extra physical contact in practice, but it gave me a much more realistic, game-speed picture of how defensive backs might react to my throws."

Still discussing a player's need to thoroughly understand the game, Don Matthews cites Doug Flutie as an example. "We were playing in Winnipeg when I was coaching the B.C. Lions in the 1980s. Winnipeg's defence blitzed one play. While scrambling for his life, Doug noticed that no one was assigned to cover our running back, Robert Drummond, as [the Winnipeg defence] must have assumed he would be required to block. When he got back to the huddle, Doug told everybody to do the same thing on the next play. He then went to Robert and told him to miss his blocking assignment and look for the ball as soon as possible. On that next play, he read the blitz perfectly, dumped the ball off to Robert, who went untouched to the end zone." The level of understanding needed to be able to design and execute that type of play is reserved for only a very few — the truly great ones.

Confidence, Courage and Commitment

If there is one characteristic you want the person playing beside you on a football team to possess, "mental toughness" may be it. You want someone who has the confidence to take calculated risks at important times in big games. You want a person who can play with pain, respond positively after a big play goes against him and rise to the top in difficult situations. Most importantly, you want the person playing with you to have made a total commitment to the game, to be prepared to do whatever is needed to win.

Pringle brought the same indomitable spirit to every situation, every game, throughout his thirteen-year career.

THINK ABOUT IT!

Ron Lancaster looks for players with a high degree of self-awareness. "What we are hoping for as a coaching staff," he explains, "especially with young inexperienced players, is that they are smart enough to know what they can't do — and committed enough to take what they know they can't do and work on it to become better."

If there is one characteristic you want the person playing beside you on a football team to possess, "mental toughness" may be it.

Mike Pringle was one of the toughest players ever to put on a helmet in the CFL. His ability to play the second half of any game at a higher, more intense level than the first half was not lost on his teammates. Bryan Chiu, his centre for seven years in Montreal, remembers what it was like: "We were playing in Toronto on their old artificial turf. Mike had broken free through the defensive line, losing his helmet in the process, and was heading down the sideline. He was met by a number of defenders and, disregarding his own safety, dragged them along for ten or more yards. When they finally did get him down, they proceeded to drag his bare scalp along the turf for a number of yards, producing a huge abrasion. Mike adjourned to the sideline, got patched up and proceeded to play with a level of intensity that inspired the rest of us. He went on to gain 170 yards in the second half, ending up with a total of 250 rushing yards. Unbelievable, the mental toughness of that man."

Pringle suffers a serious carpet burn
on his head during a 1998 game against
the Argos. But that didn't stop him
from getting patched up and coming
back into the game with a vengeance,

Calvillo (top) orchestrates the Alouettes offence.

"The most effective quarterbacks create this aura around them that sends a signal that they will get it done." – Damon Allen

Edmonton's Hall of Fame middle linebacker Dan Kepley showing his serene side — a side he almost never displayed on the field. Kepley is probably one of the top five linebackers ever to play in the CFL.

The coaches I talked to agree that another attribute the players who are mentally tough acquire is a level of confidence that is an essential constituent of greatness.

Damon Allen, a future Hall of Fame member and seemingly ageless quarterback of the Toronto Argonauts, has compiled a staggering total of 11,702 rushing yards in his career (so far). He says, "I feel I am good at making decisions and have confidence in my abilities. Why stay in the pocket when your protection is breaking down? Why look for additional receivers when a running lane opens up? The most effective quarterbacks create this aura around them that sends a signal that they will get it done, and I take pride in my ability to produce when I have to. Leadership from a quarterback emanates from the belief that the eleven other guys in the huddle believe you can get it done."

Montreal quarterback Anthony Calvillo, prior to the 2005 Eastern semi-final against the Saskatchewan Roughriders, gave a vivid demonstration of the kind of commitment the coaches were talking about. In the course of a players-only meeting, he asked the rest of his teammates to follow the example he planned to set the next day. His performance in the first half of the game that followed was awe-inspiring, and his teammates, in turn, played an inspired game. The Alouettes won convincingly: 30–14.

Derrell "Mookie" Mitchell, following his record year in 1998 with the Toronto Argonauts (he had an unbelievable 160 pass receptions), struggled at the beginning of the 1999 season. "We were playing in Hamilton, and I dropped the first three or four balls thrown to me. I had no explanation for this behaviour. Our quarterback, Jimmy Kemp, came to me and told me that he needed me in this game, [and told me] that he was going to continue throwing the ball to me. This allowed me to refocus almost immediately, and from then on it was if I had never dropped a ball." Mitchell has consistently demonstrated that he possesses the mental toughness to come back after bad plays. In 2005, after nine years in the league, he is still contributing in a big way.

Hugh Campbell says, "Greatness is really getting the most out of oneself. Getting the maximum performance out of an individual, within the team concept. There are not many individuals [like this], and only the great ones leave everything on the field year in and year out. Our great middle linebacker of the seventies and eighties, Dan Kepley, was one of these players."

Considered small and slow, Darren Flutie (82) proved that with an extraordinary level of confidence and a singular focus, the sky's the limit. He finished his career as the number two all-time leading receiver, amassing a total of 14,359 yards.

Clemons echoes this sentiment. "Great players let mistakes roll off their shoulders. If they play as a receiver and fail to make a catch, they come back to the huddle as if they had caught the ball. They return to the huddle with great confidence and the attitude that they want the ball again. It's an overwhelming confidence that seems to defy logic. Like: Why would he want the ball again when dropping it just embarrassed him? If they get the ball thrown to them on the next play they just believe — in fact, they know — they are going to catch it. The reason behind this ability to quickly re-focus is confidence, a very high level of confidence — what I call mental toughness."

Players rise to the top by demonstrating consistency, understanding and toughness over the course of a football career. In the pages that follow, both coaches and players explain in their own words how greatness emerges, beginning early in life, and continues to develop throughout an entire football career. I will try to show how greatness shows up on the field, not just in the obviously great plays, but also in the kinds of details that make a huge difference on the line, in the backfield, at every position. All three of the elements of greatness discussed here reveal themselves time and again in the everyday performance of the great players of the Canadian Football League.

2

With Both Your Heart and Your Mind

It is widely acknowledged that it takes about ten years of dedicated, focused practice to achieve a significant level of expertise in any sport. CFL players generally begin their football career in their early teens or even earlier. Most play the game either in the community or in high school and go on to highly structured college or university football programs. Rookies in the CFL are rarely younger than twenty-two years old. The ten-year rule is very seldom broken.

Solitary, resilient, embattled – an old warhorse, Jay McNeil, epitomizes the strength of character common in great players.

Family support was a key factor in the development of football greats Damon Allen (9) and his brother Marcus (32).

Even CFL rookies attending their first professional training camp bring with them a whole lot of football experience. They represent the very best football players available. They have survived a decade-long weeding out process through high school, college and university programs. They form the pool of talent from which managers, scouts and coaches select the players who will, they hope, make the difference between winning the Grey Cup and merely looking forward to another year of improvement. In every group of newcomers to the CFL there are those players who grow and flourish within this environment, becoming, with time, the stars that fans and their peers recognize as truly great players.

An Early Start

Many elite players grew up playing a variety of sports, often every day, from dawn to dusk, throughout the entire year. All the players I interviewed spoke of having very supportive families that encouraged them to play and compete in organized sports. Veteran quarterback Damon Allen's dad coached baseball, so from an early age he and his four brothers all played baseball. Allen's older brothers, especially Marcus, a National Football League star and Pro Football Hall of Famer, had a big effect on his athletic development, but he says that his father "was probably the biggest influence on us, because he taught us the fundamentals of the sports that we now play."

Like Allen, Anthony Calvillo talks about the influence of his family on his early development. "I had an older brother, so I was just expected to keep up. We played everything from one season to the next – baseball, basketball, football – we were always involved in sport."

In a similar way, Winnipeg's all-star slotback Milt Stegall played all sports from an early age. "I think from about four or five years old. My father was a key influence in my development. He was insistent that I work hard and expected me to be successful. I thrived in this environment. I still think about those early influences today. I suppose I am a lot like my father now."

Montreal Alouettes all-star offensive lineman Bryan Chiu has a different perspective. "Being of Asian descent meant I grew up with very little knowledge of football or athletics in general. My father died when I was two, and my mum wanted me to go into music, which was her absolute priority." Actually, his mother viewed football as a violent sport, and he had to agree that he would graduate from university if he wanted to stay in football. Nevertheless, Chiu's mother supported him in his ambition.

Edmonton's all-star receiver Derrell Mitchell's mother also was a strong influence on her son. "My mom instilled in me the concepts of patience and level-headedness. She never lost her composure, even through tough times. She was able to fight through adversity.... I suppose I can see where I have the same personality."

"My mom instilled in me the concepts of patience and level-headedness."

– Derrell Mitchell

ABOVE Derrell Mitchell and his mother, his guiding light and foundation. The influence and support of family is evident in the development of every great player.

LEFT The culmination of Anthony Calvillo's long football development: the 2002 Grey Cup trophy and MVP award.

GETTING PHYSICAL

Football requires size, speed and strength. With
a long-term commitment to diet and training,
aspiring football players can modify the physical
characteristics they were born with — up to a
point — to meet the needs of their respective
positions. The body type and characteristics
suitable for each position are as follows:

OFFENCE

Quarterbacks Height: 5' 9"–6' 6"   Weight: 170–250 lbs
Drop passers have to be tall, possess a strong arm and be
physically tough enough to withstand the impact of regular
tackles. Scrambling quarterbacks can be smaller and more
agile. They need to be fast and possess the ability to throw
on the run.

Running backs: Fullbacks and Tailbacks (Halfbacks)
Height: 5' 7"–6' 5"   Weight: 170–265 lbs
Fullbacks are heavy, strong and powerful runners, able to
block 280-pound defensive linemen. Tailbacks are smaller,
agile, possess significant speed and often have good
leg power.

Receivers Height: 5' 8"–6' 8"   Weight: 160–260 lbs
Receivers, above all, must have great speed and the ability to
jump. They also require agility and exceptional hand-eye
coordination.

Linemen Height: 5' 10"–6' 10"   Weight: 265–370 lbs
Linemen must be extremely strong and surprisingly agile,
often with quick feet.

DEFENCE

Linemen Height: 6' 0"–6' 8"   Weight: 225–300 lbs
Defensive tackles have to be strong, possess good leg power
and have quick reactions. Defensive ends are smaller, more
agile and often extremely fast, but with considerable strength.

Linebackers Height: 5' 10"–6' 4"   Weight: 190–250 lbs
There is a wide range of physical attributes among
linebackers, depending whether they are mainly run stoppers
or pass defenders. Both must possess quickness, strength,
agility and power.

Defensive backs Height: 5' 9"–6' 3"   Weight: 170–210 lbs
Speed, agility, coordination and balance are all required for
this position, together with a high strength-to-weight ratio.

At 6' 3" and 280 pounds, Joe Fleming (76) is the prototypical CFL defensive tackle. Here he uses his speed and quickness to sweep around an offensive lineman.

> *"As far back as I can remember, I hated letting my parents, coaches and teammates down. In some ways I am motivated by fear of failure."*
> — *Mike O'Shea*

Doug (22) and Darren Flutie (82) suited up as B.C. Lions in 1991 (right). What a thrill it must have been for the Flutie family to have two sons playing professional football for the same team.

An Aptitude for the Game

Most CFL players report that they achieved a high level of proficiency while they were still young. These early signs of natural talent allowed them to play sports relatively well in comparison to other kids their age. "Everything seemed easy for me," Anthony Calvillo remarks. "I guess I had a talent for sport. Even at five years old, I played quarterback because I had the best arm.... We had a great little community league, probably eight teams of flag football. Back then, I remember, I was chosen to play quarterback, because I could throw the ball better then any of the other kids, so I had a lot of success and felt good about playing."

With skill comes confidence. The great receiver Terry Vaughn recalls, "I was ten years old when I first started playing organized football. The league I was in was for eleven- to eighteen-year-olds, and, you know, that is a wide age margin.... I was ten, and I was right on the cut line, but I knew that if I had played with the younger kids, I would be too advanced, so I played in the older league with the older kids, you know, the eighteen-year-olds!"

One of the CFL's all-time best middle linebackers, Alondra Johnson, displayed a propensity for physical games at an early age that set him apart from his peers. "I used to break things, run into things and generally tear things up," he admits. "My whole persona revolved around a destructive pattern of behaviour.... I was always somewhat of a daredevil as a kid, jumping off roofs, doing silly things." Fortunately, he started playing Pop Warner football in Gardena, Louisiana, when he was ten. He just loved the game. His size allowed him to play with kids who were older than he was. At the same time, he says, "I caught on right away. I guess my natural talent shone through. I liked it right away. I loved to hit, and in football you could hit people and not get into trouble. That was a real revelation to me – and it still is. I have always liked the physicality of it, and I still do!"

Almost all the great players tell a similar story. Their parents and family members provided them with opportunities and support, both emotional and financial, that gave them confidence to participate and compete in sports. Their confidence motivated them to develop a strong work ethic and a determination to succeed. This determination caused them to practice hard, and practice naturally enhanced their skill. Their superior skill, in turn, led to greater achievement – which increased their confidence. The process forms a circle that builds success.

Johnson "enjoying" his sport, as he crunches Hamilton's Archie Amerson.

You can't make catches like this without a little practice. Ben Cahoon
goes vertical to introduce himself to this particular football

Mike Pringle is nothing if not a fierce competitor.

A Passion for the Game

A common thread that connects every great player is the obvious love of the game that they possess. Many speak of spending countless hours playing and practicing their favourite sports. For example, Calvillo remembers, "I lived at the park, morning, noon and night. My mom always knew where she could find me. I loved to be out there."

Allen and his brothers spent many hours pretending that they were pro athletes who were actually playing in big-league games. "We would watch some of our favourite heroes on TV, and if they played in the mud that day, we would muddy down the field with a hose, put on our uniforms and go crazy."

In grade ten, Ben Cahoon and a close friend decided to catch 500 balls per day for the whole summer. "We would stand facing each other, sometimes as little as ten yards apart, and throw all sorts of balls at each other. We would make one-handed catches, high, low, off-balance catches. The game was to try and catch every single ball, not letting any ball touch the ground. That exercise gave me confidence. I learned how to catch any ball, and I suppose, over the years, I have never met a ball that I haven't caught before."

REMEMBERED ADVICE

Mike Pringle's modus operandi for thirteen years was to run as hard as he could on every play. "My earliest role model, and a very influential one, was my boyhood teammate Deskin Goodwin. We had to play hard when Deskin was around, because if we didn't, he would get on our backs and make our lives miserable.... All through my football life I worked hard; I felt I had to, to be at my best. The most significant piece of advice Deskin offered to me – and I remember it like it was yesterday – was to run like there is nobody out there but you."

Jamal Powell (60) of the Lions gives his teammate Geroy Simon (81) a congratulatory hug after Simon scored a touchdown during a 2005 game.

The game of football, with its focus on team play, provides an exciting environment that is both physically and mentally challenging for aspiring athletes. Given the right combination of good coaching and committed teammates, youthful players can develop a real love of the game. B.C. Lions offensive lineman Jamie Taras played all kinds of sports as a youngster, but, he says, "the minute I started to play football, I felt at home on the football field more than with any other sport. I knew that this was the sport for me, mainly because of the camaraderie and a real feeling of team support."

Terry Vaughn expresses a similar sentiment when he explains why he chose football over baseball. "I just loved the physical aggression that took place on the football field, and I didn't get that with baseball. You know, I got money thrown at me for baseball, and people said, 'That is what you should play, that is what you are best at.' But it didn't hold the challenge for me. I liked the camaraderie with the guys in football, more so than in baseball. Football players are completely different from guys who play baseball. It is not the same, the camaraderie is not the same, the humour is not the same, all of that is different – it really is. I think that football is probably a little more macho, I guess, and more aggressive, and I liked that."

Show Me How

When it comes to real excellence, the ten-year rule is only the beginning. All players who ultimately reach the CFL have been through a long developmental process and have achieved a high level of expertise. What next begins to differentiate the good players from the truly special ones are their willingness to learn and their desire to be the best.

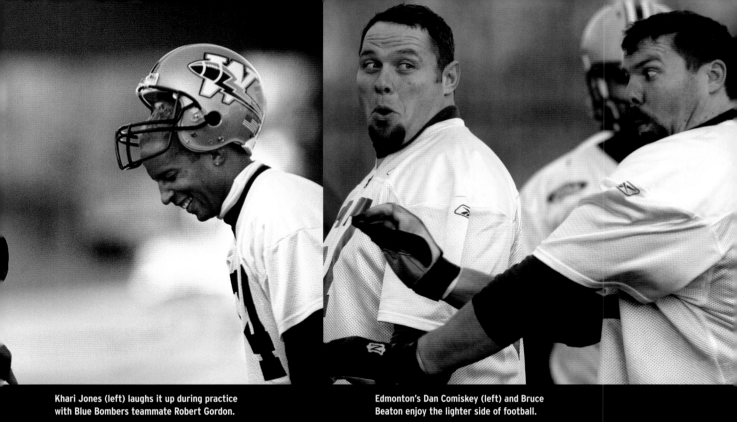

Khari Jones (left) laughs it up during practice with Blue Bombers teammate Robert Gordon.

Edmonton's Dan Comiskey (left) and Bruce Beaton enjoy the lighter side of football.

In football, there is always more to learn. Every coach and player I spoke to says that the need for improvement is an absolute requirement for achieving greatness. They also recognize this process is endless, and as young players on the threshold of their professional careers, they all regarded the great players of their time with awe and worked hard to emulate them.

Slotback Travis Moore, who has had successful stops in Calgary and Saskatchewan, admits that when he came into the CFL, "it was 1994, and I was very cocky and arrogant. I wanted to play and thought I could get it done. I thought I was ready to step right in, but with veterans like Allen Pitts and Dave Sapunjis, Will Moore and [Demetrious] "Pee Wee" Smith, there was no room for me, so I was put on the practice roster. I didn't sulk or pout like some of the hotshots I see nowadays. I took that time to learn from those guys, especially Allen Pitts."

"I felt at home on the football field more than with any other sport. I knew that this was the sport for me, mainly because of the camaraderie and a real feeling of team support." – Jamie Taras

Pitts is also mentioned by Dave Dickenson, the outstanding B.C. Lions quarterback who attributes a portion of his success to the time he spent working with Pitts during Pitts' final two years in Calgary. "I came to respect this man's vast knowledge of the game and how it is played. I learned so much from talking to him and watching him practice and play.... He really helped me to understand the passing game here in Canada."

Calvillo took a bit longer than some players to appreciate the importance of learning. He had struggled in Las Vegas and Hamilton for four years and was physically and emotionally spent after a 2-16 year in 1997. When he was signed as a free agent in 1998, Alouettes general manager Jim Popp offered him a chance to retool. He spent two years as an understudy to the great Tracy Ham, who was winding down his career. "It wasn't until I came to Montreal and got to see how Tracy conducted himself, how he went about being a professional, that I had my eyes really opened," Calvillo says. "Early on, I didn't put a lot into it in terms of the mental aspect of the game – physically either, by the way. I wasn't lifting weights during the season or during the off-season. I have really grown up as far as being a professional. I spend much more time working on my craft, both mentally and physically. He was an inspiration to me, and I owe him a lot."

Ham passed on many lessons that Calvillo has found useful over the years. One example he cites has to do with the importance of footwork. "We would do footwork drills almost every day," Calvillo relates. "In one drill, we would do this drop-back footwork for a hundred yards, rest a bit and come back a hundred yards. This really conditioned your legs, and I think your brain, so you wouldn't have to think about it in a game situation. When we got tired doing this drill, our technique would fall apart, so we had good feedback on what our technique was like.... My training plans now reflect a much clearer understanding of the key components needed by CFL quarterbacks."

Danny McManus, longtime quarterback of the Hamilton Tiger-Cats, appreciates his good fortune in having high-level mentors early in his career. "I felt that when I got to the CFL I was pretty accomplished," he says, "but I now recognize the fortunate opportunity I had early on in my career. I was a backup for five years [from 1990 to 1994 with Winnipeg and B.C.] with some of the best quarterbacks ever to play in the CFL, including Kent Austin, Danny Barrett, Matt Dunigan and Tom Burgess. What a learning environment I had fallen into, working with those players! I was like a sponge. Each one of them had a new perspective for me. I was able to understand the demands of playing quarterback in the CFL because there were five different points of view. It forced me to consider each quarterback's input and reflect on how each player looked at specific situations. It allowed me to grow and become ready to be an effective quarterback."

WHAT IS IT?

ZONE DEFENCE

Zone defence is a system of pass defence in which the linebackers and defensive backs drop to specific areas of the field rather than covering individual offensive receivers. Once deployed, they react to receivers within their area of responsibility.

MAN-TO-MAN DEFENCE

In a man-to-man defence, each offensive receiver is covered by one defensive player who is responsible for shadowing him throughout the play sequence.

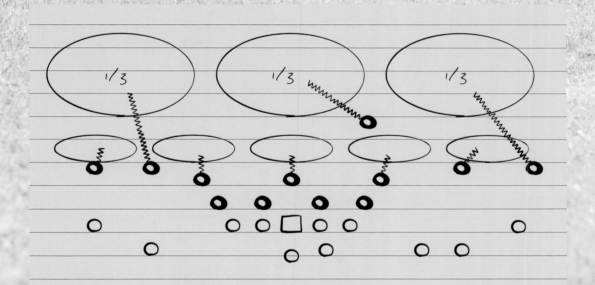

Most teams employ a zone defence of this type, referred to as a three-deep zone (with five short zones). Defenders are responsible for covering players who enter their zone.

Defensive end Joe Montford also has a story that underlines the way great players adapt to their environment effectively by having strong role models and good mentor relationships. "I remember one guy telling me that I wasn't going to be in the league long if 'you, at your weight,' were going to run into people and try to play a physical game. I ended up studying great guys in the league like Malvin Hunter [6' 3", 230 lbs] and Elfrid Payton [6' 1", 230 lbs] from Edmonton, who are considered small guys. I watched those guys, studied their moves and techniques. Jeff Cummins from Hamilton was another player who I learned from. He had great feet for a big guy and I...tried to see how he used his body position and balance to get the job done. I learned a lot from him. We worked hard together to develop our moves and to take advantage of each other's strengths."

Defensive back Marvin Coleman talks about how each player is not alone on the field. "When I first came to Calgary and the CFL, I realized very quickly that Allen Pitts and Travis Moore were exceptional football players. These two players quickly became role models for me.... I learned to understand how to play defensive back in the CFL by working with these two receivers. The type of pre-snap motion, their angle of release based on a defensive back's position, the types of breaks they used in man-to-man and zone coverages, and a million other things. Looking back, was I ever fortunate to have two of the all-time best receivers to learn from!"

WILY VETERAN

"I use coaches as one more source of feedback, not as the only source of information," says Darren Flutie. "When they tell me something, I compare it to what I know about the game and myself. I add it to my bank of knowledge. I don't accept it at face value. I am a bit of a cynic when it comes to people telling me what to do. I need to internalize it first and test it out."

Mike Clemons says that he learned a lot as a player from the defensive squad in Toronto – players like Rodney Harding, Don Moen, Doran Major, Carl Brazley and Reggie Pleasant. "These guys were such pros," Clemons recalls. "Rodney Harding, more than anyone else, taught me how to be a pro in terms of how to take care of your body, how to play with injuries, the fact that real players don't stay injured. He created an atmosphere around the facility that it wasn't acceptable to be injured. He gave people a hard time when they weren't practicing so that you came to learn to rise up to this type of challenge."

Whether it was in high school (Vancouver College, opposite, 72) or fifteen years later as the CFL's Most Outstanding Lineman, Chiu's look of determination is indicative of his level of mental toughness.

Never Satisfied

The desire to learn and the willingness to work hard have put these special players on the road to greatness. The best players recognize the need to feed this unquestionable thirst throughout their professional careers.

Clemons, that erudite player, manager and coach, puts it best when he describes great players. "The thing that differentiates the good from the great is a desire to know and understand the game. They don't use the phrase, 'I had a good year.' They focus on continual improvement. Each goal is a stepping-stone that catapults them to the next level...."

"For me, the big thing about learning is, you take an action, you get a result and then you decide if that is the result you want," explains Jamie Taras. And if it isn't the result you want, then "you recognize your need to adjust, and the good players make the effort that is needed to change the result. That, to me, is one of the biggest parts of being a professional: to commit to doing something, to making the effort to get better."

Winnipeg Blue Bombers all-star defensive tackle Joe Fleming played with Alondra Johnson in Calgary during that team's run to the Grey Cup in 2001. Calgary got off to a 1–5 start to the season, and these two defensive stalwarts recognized that a lack of focus on the part of players was playing a major role in the team's dismal record. Fleming and Johnson called a team meeting to deal with the issue. "We told the team that the players were going to eliminate the mental mistakes, that mistakes were not going to be tolerated," Fleming says. "We made a chart, and the names of players making mental mistakes in games were posted. The coaches had nothing to do with this initiative; we felt it was critical for us to do something to change the attitude on the team. From that moment on we had a different, more focused attitude, and mistakes decreased. Players studied more film, asked more questions and paid attention, because they knew they were accountable to each other."

For professional players, eliminating mistakes is of paramount importance. Bryan Chiu states, "I take a lot of pride in the mental aspect of the game. I have very high expectations for myself. I have a very hard time accepting making any mental mistakes. Physical breakdowns I can live with, but mental ones are absolutely forbidden. I am obsessed with trying to eliminate these. At this stage in my career, I know that my main strength is my mental toughness. I will not be beaten. Even if you get the best of me on one play, you better watch out, because I'm coming after you, and I will get you."

Johnson expresses a similar sentiment. "I look at a high level of mental toughness as one of the most important aspects of a successful player. He needs to be able to play through defeat, to come back after getting beaten on a play. To have the drive to go forward, to struggle on, when you're tired or down. You need to play through your struggles."

Every player I interviewed echoes Johnson's remarks. The focused determination of these great players is a cornerstone of their success. It is not easy to get to the professional level, and it's even harder to thrive. Personally, I felt threatened every year at training camp. I always wondered whether I would be good enough to keep up with the demands of this challenging game. The great players never stop preparing themselves for the next test. They are always looking for some way to get an edge. Taras sums up this idea succinctly. "Great players have mental toughness, an ability to focus, to work at preparation, coming through when they have to, selecting the right action every time."

Mike O'Shea's words ring true about the great players never being satisfied with their performances. "Football is the one game in which you could never learn everything," he points out. "So if you are committed and receptive, you have the opportunity to get better. I have said this publicly many times: Once I stop learning something new, I'm going to quit. I love to learn and know I will never stop learning more, so I will more than likely be kicked out of football long before I learn everything there is to know."

"I will more than likely be kicked out of football long before I learn everything there is to know." – Mike O'Shea

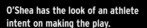

O'Shea has the look of an athlete intent on making the play.

3

Getting Ready to Compete

As the complexity of the game grows and the demands of competition increase, so does the commitment to preparation. The great players recognize this early in their careers. They are the ones who have the drive and determination to make the most of their opportunities.

ABOVE For fifteen years in the league, the B.C. Lions' Jamie Taras understood the importance of physical conditioning.

Ottawa Renegades quarterback Kerry Joseph limbers up in preparation for another physically demanding outing.

No Time to Rest

Preparation for the upcoming season begins almost before the previous season has ended. In meetings with their coaches before the team breaks up for the winter, players are made acutely aware of what they need to do in the off-season. The best players take their off-season responsibilities seriously.

When I began my professional career with the Montreal Alouettes in 1971, very few players trained year-round. Only a handful on each team lifted weights during the season. Things have changed! Now just about everyone understands the benefits of year-long conditioning programs. As a result, today's players are generally bigger and stronger than they were in my playing days. They start fitness training early – some when they are as young as thirteen or fourteen – and stay committed to it throughout their careers.

Mike O'Shea, the veteran middle linebacker of the Toronto Argonauts, believes his off-season workout regime has been a key factor in allowing him to be productive late in his career. "I am very proud of the way I work. I don't want to quantify it or say that I work harder that anyone else, but I do work very hard. I go into most seasons believing I am going to lose my job, they are going to bring someone in, and they always do. They are always trying to find someone better, cheaper, younger.... I use this attitude as motivation to work hard in the off-season."

HOMEWORK

In addition to the game-to-game evaluations, players are usually handed an end-of-season report on their performance. Together, players and their coaches discuss the evaluations and set realistic goals for improvement in the off-season. Typical goals may be to gain ten pounds, improve the forty-yard sprint time by 0.2 seconds, or catch fifty balls four times a week. The most committed players view these goals as an opportunity to eliminate weaknesses and make their game better. Jamie Taras says, "You are always off-course as a player, making corrections to get back on course.... The degree to which you are off-course lessens the longer you play and the harder you work at staying on course."

Bryan Chiu employs a variety of training techniques. "To increase my quickness and hand speed," he explains, "I box with a coach twice a week all during the off-season. I do a lot of plyometrics [rebound work, like jumping, that is good for developing leg power]. I like to train by myself, to set goals for myself. I know what I need to do by this stage in my career, and it is a little world all to myself.... I try not to have external motivators. It is part of my mental training, to push myself to another level. I get a lot of satisfaction from the results."

Milt Stegall takes pride in his work ethic as well. "I don't know any player I have played with who, in my opinion, outworks me. I work year-round on football, the physical part in the off-season, lifting weights, running and doing drills. I like to push myself, and often my training partners, to the limit. This work ethic has allowed me to develop into a complete football player, one who is committed to the physical, tactical and mental aspects of the game."

One of the players who train with Stegall, Edmonton's standout defensive end Joe Montford, reinforces Stegall's comments. "We push each other," he says. "My off-season program is even more intense than during the season. We compete in subtle ways, mentally challenging each other to go the extra mile. When Milt feels he is at the top of his level, I push him more. We build on each other's drive in a very intense way."

To hear Montford describe it, many of the best players continue to support and encourage one another just as their families and friends did when they were young. The cycle of confidence — practice, skill acquisition, achievement, confidence — remains the foundation of their success.

Time to Put Up or Shut Up

As training camp approaches, long-serving, self-assured veterans look forward to renewing friendships with both players and coaches and to refreshing the mind and body with tasks that have become second nature. Younger players and players unsure of their current status are more anxious — for them, camp is a time to demonstrate improvement from the previous year. Then there are the rookies. This group of hopefuls is under the most pressure. They need to do something to get the coaches to notice them — and do it quickly. It seems to me, when I look back on my first training camp with the Alouettes, that one of the reasons I stuck with the team that year was that I got into regular fights during practice with Hall of Fame receiver Peter Dalla Riva. Dalla Riva was, and still is, a very feisty guy, and as a defensive back I was required to cover him in training camp. I guess the coaches noticed, and perhaps even liked, my stubborn attitude — or the way I competed against Dalla Riva.

Training camp is a time to reintroduce your body and mind to football-specific tasks. Here, a Calgary hopeful works with the blocking sled.

"I have been around football since I was six years old, and I have always been receptive to new information, to understand what the coaches wanted and the theory behind it." – *Marvin Coleman*

Greg Marshall makes sure
that the players understand
his defensive game plan.

Nowadays it is much tougher for new players to get noticed in training camp. There are only two exhibition games in the CFL's pre-season, and the entire training camp is less than three weeks. Compare this to past years, when training camp was six weeks, and there were four exhibition games. Currently, most teams use the first of the two exhibition games to look at the prospects who survived the first week of practice. But there may be as many as sixty-five players on the roster and, consequently, each player may take to the field for only a quarter of the playing time. The second exhibition game is used to prepare the starting team for the regular season. If a rookie plays only a few minutes of the second game, he should prepare himself for bad news.

Greg Marshall, who was a brilliant defensive tackle in the 1980s and is now an excellent defensive coach, comments, "With the shortness of training camp, the guys can't afford to come to camp not ready to go…. Back when I started playing in 1980, training camp was six weeks. I think we played four exhibition games. Some players, usually experienced veterans, would show up knowing they had six weeks to get ready, and that was kind of the way they gauged things. Six weeks now takes you into the third week of the regular season."

COACHING STAFF

Head Coach

Offensive coordinator
Quarterback coach
Receivers coach
Line and running back coach

Defensive coordinator
Line coach
Linebacker coach
Defensive back coach

Kicking teams coach

The head coach is obviously the boss. He normally has years of experience and often chooses to be either the offensive or defensive coordinator as well as head coach. The head coach generally oversees the entire on-field operation and is responsible for all game decisions. He is the one whose neck is on the line.

The two coordinators should be the ideas people, choosing what style of play and what schemes to use. The position coaches are the labourers. They are responsible for film breakdown, coaching technique and ensuring that the players understand the specific adjustments needed from one game to the next.

I masquerade as a know-it-all coach, messing up the Alouettes' offensive game plan board.

Picking the squad is not the only purpose of training camp. Developing team cohesion and practicing timing are no less important. Each player is handed the organization's playbook on arrival. Every team has a separate offensive and defensive playbook, often further broken down by playing unit. On offence, the positional units are the offensive line, the running backs and receivers, and the quarterbacks. On defence, the units are the defensive line, the linebackers and the defensive backs. Each of these units is usually assigned a coach who has the day-to-day responsibility of making sure all players fully understand and are able to execute their respective tasks.

Of all the criteria used to select playing personnel during training camp, the ability to understand the playbook and execute plays with the fewest mistakes is probably the one that separates players of seemingly equal ability. A player who makes the same mistake twice, especially after the coach has pointed it out, is not long for the team.

Alouettes coach Don Matthews observes, "We know very early in training camp about the status of most players. It is not very difficult because we look at everything — all aspects of camp are filmed and graded. We also constantly question them. When they make a mistake, we see on film how soon they eliminate it. This is very important to us. We need players who have the ability to learn from their mistakes. When it comes down to it, although it is not always black and white, we have a lot of data [with which] to decide if a player is mentally prepared to take the next step with us as a team player."

The supremely skilled Cahoon
makes very few mistakes of
any kind.

NO FAILING MARKS ALLOWED

All professional football clubs use grading schemes to track player progress. Player evaluations are completed at the end of every game. These evaluations are used to assess individual technique, play execution and personal effort. It is usually the responsibility of the position coaches to conduct these evaluations and to discuss them with the players in their group. Many coaches post them in the locker room. The implication is that each player's performance matters to his teammates. Players' opinions about this are mixed. Insecure players may object to it. More confident players believe, however, that they should be held accountable to their fellow players; it is the football organization's bottom line.

The partial chart below, drawn up by position coach Kevin Strasser, assesses Montreal's outstanding receiver Ben Cahoon. This chart is typical of the evaluations to which all players are subjected. Cahoon's overall rating of 65/66 (or ninety-eight per cent) is typical of the high performance standards CFL players are expected to meet. Any player whose chart records less than about eighty per cent may not have what it takes to play in this league.

NAME: **BEN CAHOON**

Montreal Alouettes – Wide Receiver Grades vs. Edmonton – Gm # 15
Total Plays: 66

#	Play Call	Coverage	Assign.	Execution	Effort	Comments
1	4W6-97	3-zone	✓	✓	*	Good depth
2	R3-971	1-man	✓	✓	✓	Nice footwork & body control
3	X spot 926	1-man	✓	✗	✓	2 yard route!!!
4	43	4-zone	✓	✓	✓	Great cutoff, just do it sooner
5	R3-54	0-man	✓	✓	*	Great hustle, pays off, eh?
			65/66	63/66	65/66	Totals

"It is a chess game out there, played by both coaches and players. The adjustments you make before and during the play determine how successful you will be."

– Joe Montford

Ottawa's defensive coordinator, Richard Harris, holds up the scout team playbook. There is very little tolerance for mental mistakes on winning teams.

Game Prep

There are eighteen regular-season games for each CFL team. These are followed (for some) by one or two playoff games and topped off by the Grey Cup. Once the regular season begins, teams and players adhere to a highly regimented schedule. From one week to the next, everything is focused on preparing to play the next opponent. Ideally, coaches want three full days of practice plus a short, pre-game walk-through to prepare for each game. Following a game, each position coach breaks down the film, analyzing and grading every player's performance in his unit. When this post-game evaluation has been completed, the coaches then begin to review film of their opponent's three most recent games, as well as the last game played between the two teams. Before the first practice session, the coaches, who have evaluated the opponent's tendencies revealed by the film, develop a plan that is presented to the players at the first meeting. Over the week, with input from players, this plan is further refined, allowing the players to feel comfortable with what they are being asked to do.

Call sheets — printed game plans for the offensive, defensive and kicking squads — are sketched out. All players are expected to assimilate the opponent-specific knowledge from these sheets. One of the main functions of practice is to try out these manoeuvres on the field with some of the players simulating their opponents' tendencies.

On-field Practice

The current agreement between the CFL owners and the players (represented by the players' association) stipulates that teams can ask players to work a maximum of four and a half hours a day. For most teams, this period is divided between a pre-practice meeting of one to two hours and on-field practice sessions of two to two and a half hours. The on-field practice sessions are highly structured, more demanding mentally than physically and require players to be alert and thinking throughout.

WARM-UP (10-15 MINUTES)

There is usually a low-intensity activity period to begin practice. Often the team is broken up into position-specific groups. These units conduct a walk-through, highlighting aspects of the proposed game plan. Following this activity, the whole team does some light warm-up exercises followed by a stretching routine.

GROUP-SPECIFIC PRACTICE SESSION (15-20 MINUTES)

Five or six different groups (defensive backs, linebackers, defensive line, offensive line, running backs, quarterbacks and receivers) conduct position-specific drills. This segment is the only time that a coach has to work with his group on technical skills specific to that position.

COMBINED GROUPS (15–25 MINUTES)

The next session usually brings two or more groups together – for example, the offensive and defensive linemen, the receiver working against the defensive backs, the running backs against linebackers. Linemen might work to refine blocking schemes, for instance, and then the defensive line will employ its rush patterns against the offensive line's simulations of the opponent.

TEAM PRACTICE (30–40 MINUTES)

The entire offence runs twenty to twenty-five plays against the simulated defence of the opposing team. The procedure is then reversed: the defence tries out its game plan against an offence simulating opposition tendencies.

KICKING TEAMS PRACTICE (20–30 MINUTES)

Most players are expected to participate, either as a member of one of the kicking teams or as part of the scout team, simulating the opponent's plays. Some coaches run segments of the kicking practice – punt team, punt-return team, kick-off team, kick-off return team, field-goal team and field-goal defence team – in between other segments of the practice.

These weekly practice sessions are critical for both players and coaches, so that going into the next game they are confident and comfortable with the proposed game plan. Don Matthews, the guru of current CFL coaches comments that "players are required to understand opponents' tendencies, recognize formations, be able to check from one defence to another and in general thoroughly understand what we want to do in each and every situation. Quite sophisticated, really."

Film Study

In no other sport do players put as much time and effort into watching and analyzing film. There are approximately sixty to eighty separate offensive plays in a game, each one separated by thirty to sixty seconds. This structure leaves room for a tremendous amount of planning and strategizing. The analysis of both your own team's performance and that of your opponent plays a huge role in game preparation. Because of this, each CFL team employs at least one full-time video coordinator. He puts in endless hours filming and then editing plays in practice and game situations. The games are recorded from two angles: one from the sideline, where all players must appear in the screen, and a second view from the end zone, where only the internal linemen must be shown. The other eight CFL teams all get copies of the game films.

The video coordinator is also responsible for providing separate, edited game films, highlighting the offensive, defensive and kicking game for each position coach. On top of that, he provides copies for as many as twenty or thirty players who might opt to study game film at home.

The B.C. Lions head onto the field
for a stretch before practice.

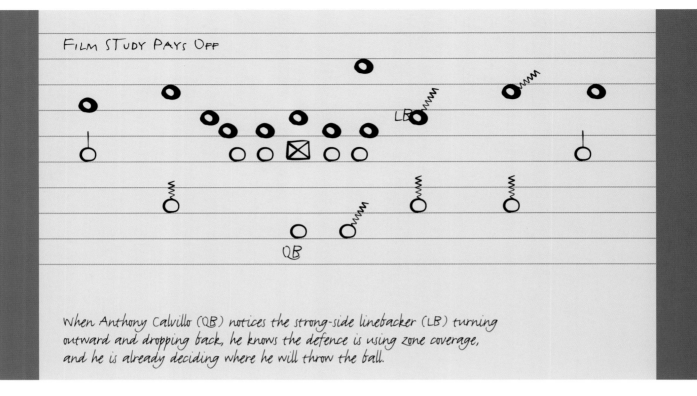

FILM STUDY PAYS OFF

When Anthony Calvillo (QB) notices the strong-side linebacker (LB) turning outward and dropping back, he knows the defence is using zone coverage, and he is already deciding where he will throw the ball.

And what do players and coaches do with the film? The primary use is for analysis. When studying an opponent, the initial focus is on discerning their overall scheme, formations and tendencies. When breaking down an opponent's film, coaches record every play, the down and distance gained or lost, the location on the field and the time remaining on the clock. They make a note of the opponent's defensive formation, the blocking scheme, the pre-snap motion, the receiver's routes and the quarterback's movements. All of this data may be fed into a computer program with integrated formulas and variables intended to yield some indication of a strong tendency that can be either countered or exploited.

The coaches use the resulting data to develop a game plan. The analysis is discussed with players at the first weekly meeting, where the coach points out key elements of the game plan while running relevant film of the opposing team.

Players use the film the same way coaches do, but they also look for their opponent's position-specific tendencies. For example, a linebacker may want to know what the formation is when an opponent is likely to run a draw play. He wants to see whether he can get a pre-snap read on that play. He may then take the analysis to another level. He may look to see whether any offensive individual gives away the play by a gesture or stance. Gordie Judges, a teammate of mine

Everything during training camp, practice and games is caught on tape, hence the phrase, "The eye in the sky doesn't lie."

THE FILM BUFF

"When you drop back as a quarterback, you have got to trust your film work – trust what you saw on tape and take it with you out on to the field," maintains Anthony Calvillo. "When I am dropping back, and I see this specific defender in a certain position, I immediately confirm that they are in zone coverage because I have recognized his technique or his drop angle from the film. You can get in a game situation and everything is unfolding as you anticipate, and at these times it is relatively simple to make plays. You do not hesitate to throw because you can trust your reads, and your level of confidence carries you along."

The Argos receivers go through their paces at the team's training facility. With so much inevitable monotonous repetition in weekly physical preparation, individual mental preparation often makes a significant difference.

with the Alouettes, a fourteen-year warhorse of the defensive line, spent countless hours studying opposition linemen on film. He once noticed that one particular lineman would put three fingers on the ground whenever he was drive-blocking and only two fingers when pass-blocking. This knowledge allowed Judges to get a jump on this opponent for years.

Players also use film to analyze their own performances. Almost all players want to see the game film the day after it was played, to learn from their mistakes and revel in their accomplishments. The great wide receiver Darren Flutie suggests that he prepares best when he watches only his own performance. "I spend most of my film-time watching and critiquing my own performance. I want to know, to confirm, what I was thinking when I ran my pass routes. When running

routes, I am constantly thinking, deciding when and how to make breaks, when to 'sit down' in zone defences, or recognizing single or double coverage. By watching the game film the next day, I check to see if I was accurate in my thinking at the time. This is a big help to me in learning to be a better receiver, [learning] how to take advantage of a particular defensive back or a specific situation. If, in watching film, I can confirm what I was thinking about a particular situation, then this builds confidence in my execution."

The Mental Edge

Mental skills, such as goal-setting, focused practice and film work, are all aspects of football preparation that players use regularly. Many of the great ones also use other forms of mental preparation such as visualization.

Visualization is a process of focused thought. Players isolate themselves and concentrate on specific aspects of their upcoming performance. Bryan Chiu says, "On game day I like to lie in bed with my eyes closed and visualize each play, often against many different sets, and even anticipated player reactions. Ultimately my goal is to accurately see the defensive players move in my hotel room and then see the same movements come to pass at game time. What a rush that would give me – imagine! Time would go so slow; you would be able to be one step ahead of every player. I make sure I visualize mostly positive things. I don't spend much time thinking about the things or movement patterns that could go wrong. Getting up for a game shouldn't be based on your insecurities or paranoid expectations."

"We need players who have the ability to learn from their mistakes.... Although it is not always black and white, we have a lot of data [with which] to decide if a player is mentally prepared to take the next step with us as a team player."

– Don Matthews

Don Matthews attempts to focus his players' thoughts on key aspects of the upcoming game.

Thirteen-year B.C. Lions veteran Cory Mantyka (left) continues working to refine his pass blocking technique.

Preparation is a multi-layered process. It is a matter of long-term physical conditioning as well as the mastery of position-specific technical skills and coordinated movement patterns. Game preparation is a matter of acquiring and assimilating information including your own team's playbook and game-by-game knowledge of each opponent's strategies and tendencies. The best teams and the greatest players are rarely surprised by what happens out on the field on game day.

4

Attack! Attack!

Offensive football is not spontaneous. It is a highly structured script of coordinated movement patterns requiring both discipline and timing. Offensive success is about effective play execution. Each player is expected to carry out specific, defined responsibilities within a framework that allows for limited improvisation. The challenge faced by these warriors is to execute effectively against an opponent who is just as focused on thwarting them. The offensive team has been prepared for its task by years of physical training and endless hours of practice. More than in almost any other sport, these athletes have to be able to make good decisions, often in a split second and under enormous physical constraints. The best players make fast, accurate decisions because they know and understand the mental demands of their position and the timing and coordination needed to execute flawlessly. Position by position, from quarterback to linemen and receivers, every individual has to be totally committed to achieving a perfect command of his tasks.

Winnipeg's Milt Stegall attacks the Calgary secondary, his eyes focused on the goal line.

The Never-ending Quest

Fans generally see only the big picture of play execution, the general movement patterns, the path of the ball and then, more precisely, the receiver making the catch and running with the ball. It takes a diligent and focused fan to watch the details of line play, the blocking patterns of the backs and the routes run by the receivers. It is these less-obvious aspects of offensive execution that generally determine offensive success. Even the fantastic catches made by the receiving corps are only the end result of a complex series of decisions and adjustments made by individuals before the receiver is in position to make the catch. Nothing is as easy as it often looks. The thrilling catches a Ben Cahoon or Terry Vaughn routinely makes, game after game, are the end product of thousands of hours spent on and off the field honing their craft. This quest to be perfect, to execute every offensive play flawlessly, is one of the hallmarks of great players.

FOCUS ON THE TASK AT HAND

Danny McManus is one of the coolest customers ever to play quarterback in the CFL. His composure during games is legendary. He has an uncanny ability to keep his wits about him, whether he has just thrown his third interception or third touchdown pass. "I am much better about controlling my emotions now than I was early in my career," he admits. "Early on I blamed myself way too much, was too hard on myself, and now I realize it slowed my development. It took me a while to understand that a quarterback doesn't have much time to get the next play off, and time spent agonizing over past mistakes takes away from preparation time critical to good execution. My focus, as soon as I see what happened to the play, is to get ready for the next play. I spend my time (and there is not that much of it) thinking about the specific game situation, what plays have been effective, even the emotional state of the offensive players. Is it ever exciting when you are able to make a mental adjustment and be effective in executing the play you have diagrammed! It's like being back in the schoolyard, drawing up plays in the dirt. 'You go long, and I'll just throw it deep!'"

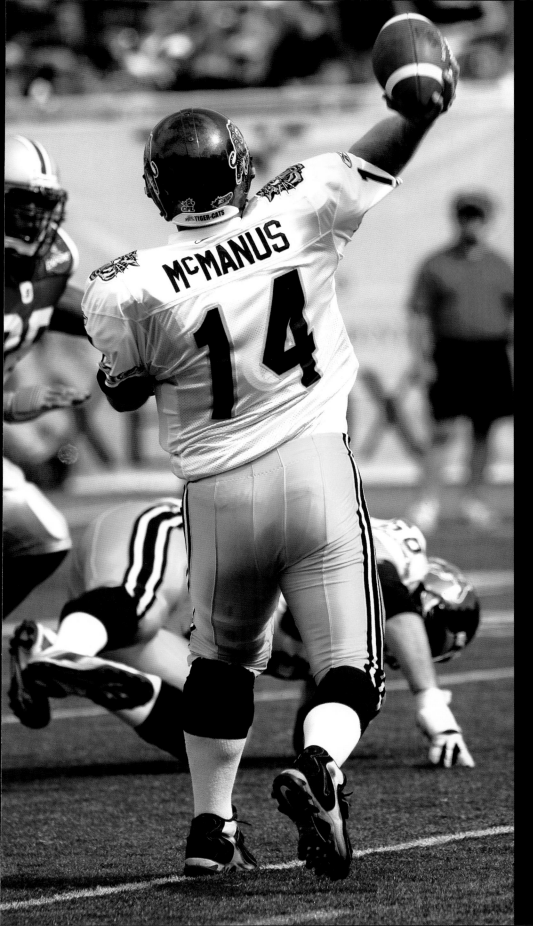

"Time spent agonizing over past mistakes takes away from preparation time critical to good execution."

– Danny McManus

McManus is famous for his on-field composure. Here he launches one to his Hamilton receiving corps.

Stegall heads up-field to find the sweet spot between the free safety and the cornerback.

COACHABILITY

Ron Lancaster explains what coaches look for when they are selecting players for their team. "You are looking to see if the player is coachable. Is he going to play the way you want him to? Is he going to be selfish? Will he take stupid penalties or cheap shots when the game is on the line? The game is physical, and you need to find players who will not hurt you with their emotions.... If you have quality players, they will control their emotions, play as physical as they can within a very strict ethical framework. There is that fine line, and if they step over it and coaches do not deal with it, you begin the slow degenerative process that will drag your team down."

FIND WAYS TO GET BETTER

Ben Cahoon's drive for perfection is demonstrated by his obsession with catching every football. "One of my key goals is to catch every single ball in every practice. If I happen to drop one, I will make sure I catch extra balls that practice. I try to focus on the last split second before the catch. It helps me with the mechanics of catching, but more importantly it helps me mentally."

Former running back Mike Pringle acknowledges that he often found new ways to develop his craft. Edmonton Eskimos head coach Danny Maciocia had an especially strong influence on his game when he was Pringle's coach in Montreal. "I think I played and ran with the ball instinctively for the first half of my career, but when I teamed up with Danny...I really started to study film and I began to appreciate offensive football from a much broader perspective. I admit that my eyes were opened to new things, like where blocks were originating from and developing, and how defences

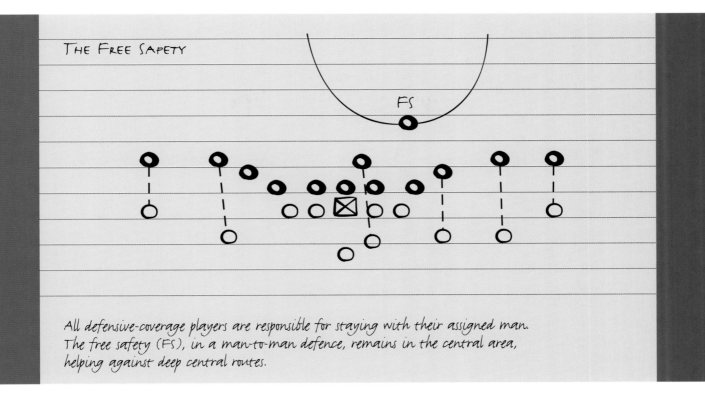

THE FREE SAFETY

All defensive-coverage players are responsible for staying with their assigned man. The free safety (FS), in a man-to-man defence, remains in the central area, helping against deep central routes.

react to offensive movement. In 2000 I had probably the best year that I have ever had [1,778 rushing yards, 5.5-yard rushing average, 19 touchdowns]. I know I had been coached about these aspects of offensive football, but it seemed like I thought that perhaps it didn't apply to me, that somehow I was bigger than this type of detail. Looking back on my career, it is just amazing to me that I did as well as I did with what I now realize was a limited package."

Milt Stegall has gained 12,318 yards as a receiver in eleven years of playing with the Winnipeg Blue Bombers, but it wasn't until his eighth year that he produced his most impressive numbers. He was chosen the CFL's Most Outstanding Player in 2002, the year he amassed 1,862 receiving yards and caught an amazing twenty-three touchdown catches. "It took me a while to learn to account for the free safety on defence, but now I love to challenge that position." The free safety in the CFL is usually aligned much deeper than the other defensive

backs and is centrally located among the receiver group. In zone situations he is lurking, patrolling the centre of the field for unsuspecting receivers, waiting to blast them out of the game when they run blindly across the field on post or crossing routes. Stegall learned to focus on the free safety, adjusting his route-running to take advantage of his speed in situations where the safety was misaligned or had a blitz responsibility. He has become the acknowledged expert of the deep seam route and continues to be a terror to free safeties throughout the CFL.

These great offensive players recognize that they are in a continuous battle with defensive opponents who are doing their best to disrupt the execution of beautifully designed offensive plays. They grudgingly acknowledge that they are not going to win every battle, but their competitive instincts mean that they never stop fighting.

Timing and Coordination

The key to effective play execution is for all the offensive players to go about their assigned tasks in a coordinated, seamless fashion. They need to recognize how they fit into the overall scheme and how their movements will affect the entire play. Coaches begin this process by preparing the framework so that the players have common ground from which to work. The playbooks contain dozens of offensive plays, each one part of a system designed to take advantage of defensive weaknesses. The practice sessions are designed to allow individuals and units to work out the kinks in effective execution. The variables that need to be considered, especially when you factor in the numerous defensive possibilities, are endless. The coordination of the offensive plays requires continuous on-field adjustment, mostly because the defensive players don't stay put. It would be a lot simpler for CFL offences if the defensive players were not allow to move but, of course, this is not the case. The ever-changing reality of the defensive response to offensive movement means that the offensive players must be diligent in their pursuit of the perfect play, recognize the need to work effectively with their teammates and develop a deep understanding of their role in the system.

ONE UNIT, ONE PURPOSE

The seamless coordination of the offensive line, more than any other single factor, determines the outcome of each offensive play. One false step, one split-second delay, even one missed body-language cue from a teammate, usually means that the play will falter.

The oldest players on every team in the league are offensive linemen. There's a reason for this. Coaches know that they need to keep these units together. Veteran offensive linemen have such a store of knowledge about football and about each other that communication among them often isn't even verbal. Bryan Chiu went even further, saying, "If you are still at the level where you need to make verbal calls to get the coordination right, you will invariably be a step too slow to win many of the battles. You need to fine-tune your play to where it is almost instinctive." Uzooma Okeke, Chiu's teammate for the past ten years, agrees. "One reason I don't talk too much during the game is that it is more important for the adjustment to come from the middle outwards to me, to have one central captain who relays information on. When watching film you can see this flow of action, but only if you are an offensive lineman. The subtlety of movements would be missed by anyone except the offensive line players and their position coach. Not even the other players on the team could appreciate the coordinated movements needed to be a great unit. All anyone else sees is the running back being great or the quarterback making beautiful throws. But *we* know!"

"If you are still at the level where you need to make verbal calls to get the coordination right, you will invariably be a step too slow to win many of the battles."

— Bryan Chiu

The Als' Okeke "ties up" with a Renegade.

Gene Makowsky's eyes tell of a single-minded determination as he prepares to defend against Hamilton's attack.

RUN-BLOCKING

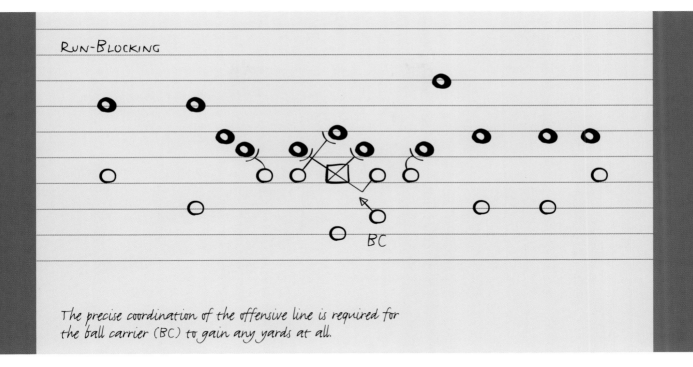

The precise coordination of the offensive line is required for the ball carrier (BC) to gain any yards at all.

Gene Makowsky and Andrew Greene, two of the mainstays on Saskatchewan's current impressive offensive line, have been working out the kinks together for eight years now. "On the football field we pretty well act as one, very seldom talking to each other," remarks Makowsky. "I trust him implicitly and I know whatever I do will be OK with Andrew, as he will be able to read me just as easily as I read him." Makowsky brings up the 1997 Western final against Edmonton, where Saskatchewan's offensive unit was virtually perfect. "We so dominated Edmonton's defensive line that we never allowed them to have the ball. Our offensive line was totally synchronized and acted as if we were one player."

LINEMEN AND RUNNING BACKS

There are two types of running back: one that relies on speed and agility to set up blocks and avoid potential tacklers, and the other that relies chiefly on power and strength to generate yards. Offensive linemen adapt their techniques and blocking schemes to the particular qualities and strengths of their ball carrier.

Edmonton's twelve-year-veteran offensive lineman, Bruce Beaton, says, "I find it much easier to block for a back who has great speed. John Avery, playing in Edmonton in 2002, was speed personified, and I feel he made my job a lot easier. When he took the ball and attacked the outside, the defensive end had to widen much faster to cut him off. That allowed me to attack my defender directly, and then John could cut off my block. If you are blocking for a slower back, the defensive lineman can wait a little bit, putting you in a dilemma, not knowing exactly which way to take the defender."

Chiu, on the other hand, loved blocking for Mike Pringle, who was power personified. "The 1998 season was like a year-long highlight reel for our 'O' line. Mike got his 2,065 yards [a CFL record for yards in a single season], and we knew it was as much our record as his. Mike was a 'downhill' running back. He hit the hole at full speed, and we knew the timing of each play to perfection. Plus I feel I have more in common with a back that is physically dominant and not afraid to get his nose a little dirty. With an attitude like that he becomes an extension of the offensive line, and we can revel in his success."

Danny McManus, known for his quick release, has already chosen his target.

WHAT IS IT?

SET UP

A sequence of events in which a player begins to move in a way that is meant to force his opponent to adjust, allowing the player to make a second move that may take advantage of this adjustment. For example, a running back might set up his offensive lineman's block with a fake and then use a change of pace to take advantage of this situation.

A SPECIAL RELATIONSHIP

The timing and coordination of the passing game are probably the most difficult aspects of offensive team play. When you consider the space between the quarterback and his potential receivers, combined with the exacting demands of the receivers' routes as they move among the defenders, you can begin to appreciate the difficulties the players confront. Each team has from four to seven potential receivers. The quarterback must develop a level of trust with these individuals, and because there is only one ball, it is unlikely the level of trust will be equal among all receivers. Virtually every quarterback has at least one favourite receiver, the player who ends up with most of the team's catches and who, more importantly, makes many of the big-play catches that successful teams require.

Ben Cahoon and Anthony Calvillo have been teammates with the Montreal Alouettes for nine years, and throughout that time they have developed a special on-field relationship. "Anthony knows that it doesn't need to be a perfect throw for me to be able to come down with the ball," Cahoon points out. "Anthony

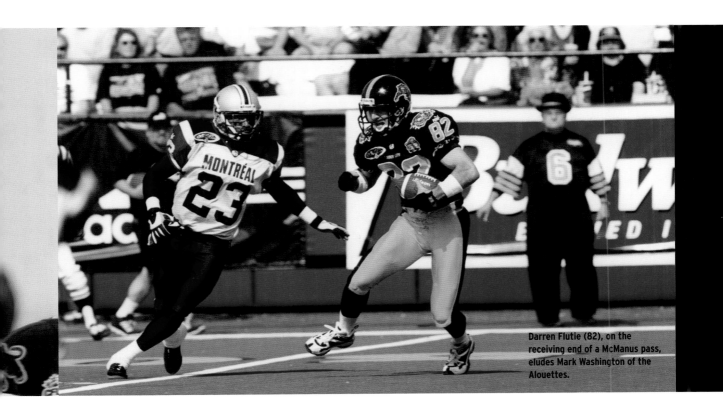

Darren Flutie (82), on the receiving end of a McManus pass, eludes Mark Washington of the Alouettes.

and I recently had a discussion about that, and he finished off the conversation by saying that he would know when to throw the ball based on my body language.... Against Ottawa in pre-season there was a play where it broke down and Anthony was forced to scramble. We receivers have scramble rules, and in this case I was supposed to turn up field and go deep. I did that, but I noticed the defensive back was in position to shut me off, so I ad-libbed and turned back to the line of scrimmage. The moment I turned around, the ball hit me in the chest. The thought went through my mind, 'How did Anthony know I was going to do that?' I asked him later. He smiled and said that he knew me, and I wasn't going to beat anyone going deep. He sensed that I knew that as well, and his timing was perfect."

Danny McManus and Darren Flutie played together, first in Edmonton and then again in Hamilton, for a total of seven years. This relationship was instrumental in Flutie becoming the second all-time leading receiver in the CFL. McManus acknowledges the value of working so long with a professional like Flutie. "I have

thrown so many balls to Darren, both in practices and games, that I know him inside and out. He is my all-time favourite receiver.... I have confidence in him. Not only in his ability to catch the ball, but also to run the route that's needed to get open, to make the move at the right time and to come through in the clutch. It has taken literally thousands of throws to get where we are now. I know his moves, how he sets up his moves, when he is going to add a second move, and everything about him on the football field. There have been countless times when I have thrown the ball to him on instinct, hoping that he will make the move I expect him to make, long before he has his head around to look for the ball. Most of those times we have been successful, and each time there is success it builds a stronger bond and reaffirms the confidence we have in each other. It is probably one of the greatest things about playing team sports, developing that special feeling for your teammates. No one can take away that feeling or that sense of unity."

Milt Stegall and Khari Jones played with the Winnipeg Blue Bombers in 2002 and shared a similar affinity. "You need to be on the same page as the quarterback if you want to be successful," maintains Stegall. "It is a lot more than just running the route assigned to you in the playbook. You need to have the same clock in your head as the quarterback has, to know when he is running out of time, when to look for the ball and a million other little details. Sometimes during a game, or even for part of a season, you are in complete sync with your quarterback, and you just know when you are going to get the ball. You get a sense that there are just two of you playing this game. In 2002, the year I won the league MVP award, Khari Jones and I were on the same page of the playbook almost every game. He threw for a league-leading forty-six touchdowns and I was the recipient of an amazing twenty-three of them. Even though the opposing teams knew that I was the favourite receiver and did everything they could do to prevent us from teaming up, we had such chemistry between us that Kahari continued to throw me the ball."

The superb B.C. Lions quarterback, Dave Dickenson, feels that his receiver Geroy Simon's level of confidence has made their relationship an easy one to develop. "I admit there are times that I rely on [Simon] to get the job done. He doesn't let me down very often. One time versus Toronto, in a game in 2005, the defensive blitz caught me off-guard, and I didn't have time to look around. I knew Geroy was running a deep seam route, and I just flung it deep in his direction. He made an unbelievable catch and took it in for the score. It is pretty easy to develop confidence with a receiver when he makes plays like that."

Offensive Skills

Every football player tries to carry out his responsibilities. He follows the coaches' instructions and understands his role in each offensive play. His athletic ability gives him the capacity to fulfill the demands of his position, but it is his mental capacity to understand the subtleties of effective play execution that separates the good from the great. All football players who make it to the CFL are good athletes with exceptional skills. The ones who develop into special players are the ones who deepen their own understanding of the game and the factors that influence performance at their position. All quarterbacks can throw the football, but knowing when and where to throw the ball is really the key to passing success.

CONTROL UNDER PRESSURE

Over the last twenty-six years, the CFL's Most Outstanding Player Award has been given to a quarterback eighteen times. No other player touches the ball as often or has more power to decide the fate of his team. And since the CFL began its evolution from a running to a passing league in the late 1970s, the quarterback, through the use of his passing arm, is required to execute the bulk of the offence.

Damon Allen has been the consummate professional quarterback for twenty-two years, and from every perspective he exudes the impression of being the man in control. "You are always taught as a quarterback to be composed and calm so that you can demand the attention of your team," says Allen. "When things are chaotic, you must be at your most relaxed, because

*"I find it easy to play
this position. I spent a
lot of time preparing
to play the game,
to put myself in a
position to be able to
make good decisions."*

– Damon Allen

everyone is looking at you, and when you are relaxed there is a calmness you bring among the other players. When you lose it in the huddle, everything goes crazy."

Allen takes a lot of pride in his ability to remain poised in difficult situations. He feels that his vast experience in the game has allowed him to deal with the various situations that routinely present themselves. "I understand the big picture well; I always have. I find it easy to play this position. I spent a lot of time preparing to play the game, to put myself in position be able to make good decisions. I feel this aspect of the game is one of my strengths." When it is suggested to him that he has become the focal point of his team's offensive schemes by utilizing shovel-pass plays, pass-run option plays, quarterback options, Allen agrees. "During the 2000 Grey Cup game in Calgary we were playing the Montreal Alouettes, and they had an aggressive defence. We knew we had to show them new things they had not seen before, to try to throw them off their game. We had been running the shovel pass all year, and I felt we needed a change-up to that play. I felt so confident and in control that we decided to use the wide receiver as the shovel man." This takes an amazing amount of coordination, as the wide receiver needs to motion in from the wide field position and Allen needs to anticipate the timing perfectly. "I think we ran that play twice in the Grey Cup game, both for gains. I really felt I was at the top of my game that day." The B.C. Lions won the Cup that year, and Allen demonstrated once again his level of control under pressure.

Dickenson in the tricky process of accurate decision-making under pressure.

WHAT IS IT?

SHOVEL PASS

The quarterback begins the play from the shotgun formation by rolling out to one side with the running back running parallel to him, but closer to the line of scrimmage. The running back waits for the quarterback to toss him an underhanded pass as the defensive end attacks the quarterback with the ball.

PASS-RUN OPTION

This play is designed to give quarterback two choices as the play develops. With the ball, the quarterback usually rolls out either to his left or to his right, and he chooses to throw to a receiver or run on his own, depending on the reactions of the defensive personnel.

QUARTERBACK OPTION

The quarterback receives the ball from the centre and quickly moves parallel to the line of scrimmage, intending either to run or to lateral the ball to a waiting running back. The back is poised to receive a lateral pass when and if the quarterback chooses to toss him the ball.

"My learning curve was slow and steady.
With learning comes confidence."

– Ron Lancaster

Scroll forward four years to the 2004 Grey Cup in Ottawa, where Allen's Toronto Argonauts met his old team, the B.C. Lions, in a match where Allen once again proved he was the man in control. He orchestrated an offensive game plan that continually had the Lions off-balance. He looked and played like a much younger man, effectively using his running skills in key situations that sustained important drives. "I was always looking to throw first, but this was dependent on the amount of time I thought I had. Even on a rollout or sprint action, if the pressure was not in my face, I scanned the field looking to find open receivers. But when the protection broke down or the receivers were covered, I was confident I could get the needed yards by running."

Allen is the longest-serving quarterback in the history of the CFL, and Ron Lancaster is not far behind. Lancaster played for nineteen productive years, first with Ottawa and then with Saskatchewan. I was fortunate (or possibly unfortunate!) in that I played against his Saskatchewan Roughriders for eight years until the end of his career in 1978. During that time, every game against his team was tough. He was called the "Little General" because he could command the field, choosing plays that were least expected. He made difficult throws seem commonplace and almost always kept his team in the game down to the last play.

Fresh-faced Lancaster from his rookie year in Ottawa, biding his time and learning from the legendary quarterback Russ Jackson.

"A major factor that helped my development was the fact that George Reed played in Saskatchewan at the time," Lancaster says. "One year in the mid-1960s, our offence had almost the same number of yards rushing as we did passing. I knew George was going to get his yards – it was a given – and this took much of the pressure off me. I acknowledged that I didn't have to win every game myself. This allowed me to last a long time in the league. My learning curve was slow and steady. With learning comes confidence. Once George began to slow down later in his career I was able to change my game and I had the confidence to do more things."

I have had the pleasure of working in Montreal with CJAD radio throughout Anthony Calvillo's tenure there and have come to know and appreciate his excellence first-hand. He is a quiet, unassuming individual who has worked hard to become the man in control. He recalls an incident that occurred in a game in Winnipeg against the Blue Bombers a number of years ago. "We had lost yards on first down, and I knew what play our coach then, Jim Barker, and I had prepared for that specific down and distance situation. Because it was late in the game, and we needed a scoring drive, I called a timeout and went to the sideline to talk it over with my coach. I think back on that situation and I recognize that I wasn't as confident about my preparation as I should have been and was looking for support or confirmation from my coach. I think now I wouldn't need to do that, as I have moved forward from where I was in terms of deciding on the appropriate call. I can see myself as growing, maturing as a quarterback."

Perhaps the ideal situation is one in which coach and quarterback have enough confidence in one another that the quarterback is left to call his own game. Don Matthews believes that the quarterback who calls his own plays is more accountable. "It's like being a point guard on a basketball team," he explains. "You can see everything developing and make decisions in leading the team. Doug Flutie was unbelievable and thrived in this type of atmosphere when he was in Toronto with me in 1996–97. His play choices showed a level of understanding that was amazing. I believe when a quarterback calls his own plays he is only held back by his own imagination."

QUARTERBACK VISION

Like all elite quarterbacks, Lancaster developed the ability to pick up small cues from the action on the field, usually in the middle of movement patterns that would look chaotic to most observers. The great quarterbacks learn to read movement patterns like chess moves and can predict what will happen, based on what they see, with a high degree of accuracy. "You have to be able to see things that are important without looking at them," says Lancaster. "For example, on a certain pass play, your read may be the linebacker, but you have to know where the safety is to be sure you can throw the ball, or else you can move the safety or middle linebacker with your eyes, get them to bite on a false read, so you can get them away from where you would like to throw the ball. Wilkie [former Edmonton quarterback Tom Wilkinson] and I often talk about the feeling we had, playing on days when you were in total control. You know that when that ball is snapped it seems that all hell breaks loose, people are running and hitting everywhere, but on those days you can see the receivers running through zones in slow motion, and you could throw the ball through the eye of the needle."

COACHES AND QUARTERBACKS

Damon Allen has been around so long, there's not much a new coach can show him that he hasn't seen before. "The coaches I work best with are the ones who take the approach that appreciates what I do best or can do most effectively," he says. "Once we can have that basic understanding, then hopefully he encourages me to explore the edges of my box, not to build an entirely new box. I pick up things fast, probably because I have so many experiences within my box, and it is easy to make references to past experiences."

Perhaps the ideal situation is one in which coach and quarterback have enough confidence in one another that the quarterback is left to call his own game.

OPPOSITE Wally Buono (left), B.C. Lions head coach, trying to get on the same page as quarterback Dave Dickenson — not always an easy task.

ABOVE Doug Flutie had uncanny vision. He was almost impossible to sack and was able to find receivers through efficient scrambling.

SIMPLE READS

Anthony Calvillo reveals the thoughts going through his head when he takes the snap.

"In the passing play O-77-54-stop," he says, "what I like to do is to look at one particular defensive player to give me a 'read,' to know what the defence is going to do. I would pre-select a particular player on the defence, knowing he is the critical factor against the play I've called. The 'O' in the play indicates the third widest receiver is going directly to the flat [a short pattern toward the sideline], and if the defender lined up over him runs directly with him, I've got a good indication that the defensive coverage is man-to-man. It is then a much easier process deciding when and where to throw the ball."

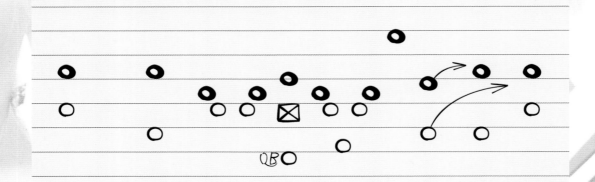

When Anthony Calvillo (QB) sees the linebacker covering the third receiver strong to the flat, he knows the defence is playing man-to-man coverage.

LAYING IT ON THE LINE

The complexity of offensive-line play is seldom fully appreciated. For example, when Bryan Chiu explains the difference between run-blocking and pass-blocking, he points out that the difference extends even to the personalities of the players involved. "These skills demand two opposing mentalities," he maintains. "In a pass offence you need to be passive, you can't dictate tempo; the defensive linemen pin their ears back and are attacking. You need to refocus your ego, take pride in other aspects of the game. It is hard for some to play this role, the protector, and not the aggressive hunter role."

Uzooma Okeke agrees with Chiu about this Jekyll-and-Hyde business. "When you are pass-blocking," he says, "you need to be able to feel good about preventing the quarterback sack, [but] when you are run-blocking, you can physically dominate an opponent. I think I am no different from most offensive linemen when I say that I would rather run-block than pass-block."

He continues, "When you are run-blocking, you are the aggressor, dictating to the defence the terms of the encounter. This psychology is reversed when you are pass-blocking. Football is a violent game, and emotion plays a big role, with intimidation and attitude being important tools for success. As a pass-blocker, you have to be more submissive, more reactive. You can't allow yourself to be very emotional about your play. Patience, timing and good technique are more important than emotion and aggression. I suppose this is one reason I have taken to becoming such an effective 'puncher': it allows me to demonstrate my aggressive, competitive nature within this context. If I can position myself accurately against a pass-rush, and if I time my punch, have enough patience, then I just love the feeling I get when I hit the opponent. It feels like a boxer making a real good, solid blow, an aggressive, attacking type of technique."

RUN-BLOCKING AND EGO

Chiu agreed with Okeke about run-blocking. "As a run offence, you can get that cocky swagger about you," Chiu muses. "It's me against you. I can tell by the way we walk to the line; we hunker down and get ready to attack. This is very ego-oriented, and some personalities are more suited to this type of offence. The more you run the ball, the more you get in that groove, especially if you are successful at it. You actually feel as if you are defeating the opponent one play at a time. It is extremely good for your ego. When Mike Pringle was our back [Alouettes, 1996–2002], we were very different than we are now, when Anthony [Calvillo] throws the ball eighty to ninety per cent of the time. For those years we took immense pride in our ability to dominate, to be physically superior, if you like. Now we have to re-orient our egos to feel good about our ability to protect Anthony, to win the team battle. It is psychologically quite different."

The Ottawa Renegades offensive line sets up, trying to keep their quarterback clean.

"I keep a book on the older, more experienced defenders, the ones who I play against regularly, to mentally prepare myself to work against their weaknesses."
— Terry Vaughn

Montreal's Terry Vaughn shakes free of his coverage and makes a difficult catch.

KEEPING THE QUARTERBACK CLEAN

Okeke may be the best pass-blocker in the CFL. Both his textbook technique and his ability to be consistent set him apart from his peers. "I have learned to keep a mental book on every opponent and note their favourite moves...and I work hard to uncover their limitations. That's the real game-within-the-game," Okeke asserts, "especially for an offensive tackle. More so than the other offensive-line positions, the tackle is most often locked in a one-on-one battle because of the outside position on the offensive line."

Gene Makowsky has played offensive tackle and guard and agrees with Okeke about the difficulty of pass-blocking the CFL defensive ends. "In the CFL the defensive ends are usually significantly lighter and faster than the defensive tackles, and as such they are much more manoeuvreable. You need to be on your toes, very focused, when pass-blocking, especially against the likes of Joe Montford and Elfrid Payton, both being known for their agility and quickness."

"I love the challenge presented by each and every defensive lineman," says Okeke. "I think I love it so much because I have now gotten to the place where I have a high level of confidence in my abilities. I know if I execute properly, I will likely win the encounter. The fun part is dealing with, and trying to solve, the problems presented by each particular opponent. I have tremendous respect for an opponent who can get me off my game by changing up his technique or doing something that he does not usually do."

GETTING INTO THE OPEN

No less than the quarterback and linemen, the relative skills of the receivers have a huge bearing on the outcome of offensive plays. Terry Vaughn has long been considered one of the premier receivers ever to play in the CFL. His competitive instincts and aggressive style of play have been instrumental in his development. "On passing plays one of the first things I do is figure out whether the defence is playing zone coverage or man-to-man coverage. This is relatively easy to do, especially with my years of experience. As the huddle breaks and I begin my early motion, I know the defensive coverage ninety per cent of the time. Zones are easy to run against once you have played in the league for a number of years, but I love playing against man.... As soon as you recognize zone coverage, you just find a hole and sit down in it. But playing against man, it's you versus your opponent, you know, it's where I make my living. Bigger defenders give me more trouble; they give everybody more trouble. They try to get their hands on you and disrupt your timing and your route. You need to develop different techniques against these players, like preventing them from getting their hands on you and avoiding contact as you release from the line of scrimmage. I keep a book on the older, more experienced defenders, the ones who I play against regularly, to mentally prepare myself to work against their weaknesses."

Moore keeping his "bag of money" all to himself.

ON BEING A PROFESSIONAL

"I am better now, in my twelfth year, at keeping up with what defences are doing," said Darren Flutie in 2002, his last year in the CFL. "There are always changes in how defences organize themselves, and sometimes at the beginning of the year they can be a little confusing. It doesn't take me long to recognize the system and the adjustments. Remember, this is my job, to get open and to make the catch. If I didn't know how to do those things and allowed the defences to have an advantage, I feel I wouldn't be earning my money. I wouldn't be a professional."

Ben Cahoon remembers a game against Calgary in which he was matched up against Davis Sanchez, a former teammate. "We were on the six [-yard line] and I knew Davis expected me to run the out pattern. I had to really sell the out, get him to bite on my move before I broke the pattern deep. It worked to perfection, Anthony [Calvillo] laying the ball in at the back of the end zone. Davis came up to me later, a big grin on his face, and acknowledged that I had won that battle with a superb pass pattern."

Another player in this elite group was Allen Pitts, the CFL's all-time yardage leader. Dave Dickenson had the good fortune to play with him over the final two years of Pitts' great career. "Because he had such a phenomenal out pattern and caught so many balls on this move," Dickenson says, "it allowed him to develop other patterns off this move. If you were a defensive back and tried to stop his out move, he would lull you into a false sense of security and, when you least expected it, would turn it up for a big play. I clearly remember that type of move during the 1999 Labour Day game in Edmonton. He waited until late in the game, setting up the play with a number of out moves, and then came to me in the huddle and said it was time to throw him the ball on an out-and-up. It worked to perfection, beating Glenn Rogers Jr. for a long touchdown reception."

PLAYING CATCH

I asked Travis Moore to explain what he thought about once he saw the ball in the air and knew it was intended for him. He says that all good veteran receivers instinctively know when the ball is being thrown to them. He sees it as a function of the quality of their route, the separation they achieve from the defender or the space they see in front of them. When he knows it's on the way, Moore then prepares himself for the next phase: making the catch. "I have this attitude that the ball is mine, it belongs to me, that I've got to have it," he explains. "I look at it as if was a bag of money, and I make sure nobody else gets it. When the ball is in the air, and I know it is coming to me, everything else is zoned out. I don't hear or feel anything, no sounds or footsteps. My concentration is so specific. I see the ball, the rotation, the flight path and the angle and that's all. The only exception is when it is a long ball and you are clear of the defender and waiting for the ball to get there. Then, for some reason, you hear everything, including the crowd noise and the defenders' grunts and breathing. You just want the ball to hurry up and get there."

POWER AND STRENGTH

Mike Pringle was the epitome of the ideal running back for thirteen glorious seasons. He ran with power and strength, relying on his natural abilities combined with a determination unmatched by any of his peers. Not since the great George Reed plied his craft in the 1960s and 1970s had we seen such an unstoppable force on a football field. He carried the ball on 2,962 occasions and caught it 396 times by the end of the 2004 football season. Most of those rushing yards resulted in significant contact, sore muscles and aching joints, both for himself and for hundreds of defensive opponents.

"I think that the running-back position is the only position on the team that you can't coach," says Pringle. "I really believe that. The only thing that a coach can do is to make you understand the designed structure of the blocking schemes. A good running-back coach will tell you where the play is designed to go, but once you get the ball, you just do what you do. A coach needs to understand the strengths of the back and design schemes to allow him to take advantage of his abilities. I've played my best football when I'm in a zone where you don't see anything but open space. Sometimes when you are playing in this zone, playing with confidence, you just see holes.

"When I am out there on the football field, I feel as if I am at home. It feels so comfortable to me. I know my role, my job, so to speak. I know I am good at what I do. And I just love the physical and mental aspect. I love to compete. I am very good at this."

THE ALL-PURPOSE RUNNING BACK

The running back's position has evolved since the late 1970s, when the Edmonton Eskimos first began using two slots backs and no tight end. The rest of the CFL responded to the Eskimos' success by turning increasingly to the passing game. Today most teams employ only one running back, and sometimes they even take him out of the offence entirely. This trend has, by extension, spawned the development of the all-purpose back: a player who can block, run the ball and be part of the passing attack.

It could be said that Mike Clemons was the living embodiment of the "all-purpose back." Check out his offensive statistics — he holds the CFL's all-time all-purpose-yards record. From 1989 to 2000, Clemons rushed for 5,341 yards and gained 7,015 yards as a receiver, 6,025 yards as a punt-returner, 6,349 yards in kick returns and 655 yards in missed field-goal returns — for a total of 25,815 yards.

"Our coach in university played a pro-style offence," says Clemons. "We played a single-back offence in which I caught sixty-eight passes my junior year and seventy passes my senior year as a running back. This experience provided a well-formed bridge to the Canadian Football League. The specific knowledge I gained in that system was totally transferable to the CFL game."

The unstoppable force that is Mike Pringle.

Being very good as an offensive player is so much more than being able to follow the diagram of the selected play or relying exclusively on instinct. The development of the specific skills needed to execute offensive responsibilities takes time, commitment and determination evident in the way men like Pringle play the game. Football skills are essential, but no less important is the intelligence required to outsmart and outmanoeuvre an opponent. The game of offensive football is played not on a chessboard, but on a field, against a violent and determined foe. The great offensive players use their intelligence to make fast, accurate decisions, putting themselves in situations that give them an advantage over their opponents. The reason they sometimes fail is that the defensive players lined up against them are just as smart, experienced and well prepared as they are.

5

No Room for Scaredy Cats

The job of the defensive player is a demanding one. Because he has no sure way of knowing what play the offensive team is about to spring, he has to be prepared for a multitude of possibilities. The more accurately he and his teammates can anticipate the upcoming play, the more likely it is that they will be able to repel the attack. Accurate anticipation is the most important skill that a defensive player must develop — it's even more important at the professional level than physical skill.

ABOVE Nasty Ed Philion, a no-holds-barred competitor, mixing it up with the crowd.

Sheldon Napastuk (left) and Dan Comiskey get up close and personal in a battle for supremacy.

Good defensive players become great when their ability to anticipate has become almost instinctive. The best believe that they almost always know what the offence is about to do. This high level of confidence comes across as an aggressive, often arrogant, attitude on the field. Alondra Johnson thrives in this world because he has complete confidence in his decisions. As he puts it himself, "There is no room for scaredy cats out there."

The Big Picture

I used to feel sorry for the rookies at training camp. Your first look at a defensive playbook is extremely intimidating. As a rookie you are faced with terminology, diagrams and position charts and adjustments that seem more like Egyptian hieroglyphs than football instructions. You quickly come to understand that your responsibilities are numerous and complex. Even with two practices each day and as many as six hours of meetings and film work during training camp, it takes a considerable amount of time before you begin to see the big picture.

Veteran players have a huge advantage in that they already know the defensive schemes and their role in each one. They spend their time developing improvement strategies, dredging up past play scenarios and filtering them through a vast array of play options. The best players make this their first priority; they thoroughly investigate every nuance of offensive schemes, seeking to uncover the reasons behind the offensive coordinators' designs and to understand all possible variations in the big picture.

One of Greg Marshall's strengths was that he respected his opponents and tried to understand the offensive schemes. "I liked to know what all the offensive players were supposed to do and how the whole thing worked together, so that I could maybe take a chance and go somewhere I wasn't designated to go. I tried to understand where the other guys were going to be and where there might or might not be an opening for myself." But, Marshall admits, "I got a rude awakening one game against Montreal, thinking that all my study and understanding was going to always go my way. They set me up and suckered me a couple of times on a bootleg type play and really took me out. I read the play and reacted to what I expected, but they had changed the blocking scheme, and I ran into a wall of blockers. They ran it three or four times before I caught on. Later on, I found out they had designed the adjustment to take advantage of the way I played, and from that day on I had a new level of respect for my opponent. I realized that the game is continually evolving, and the work needed to be on top of things is never-ending."

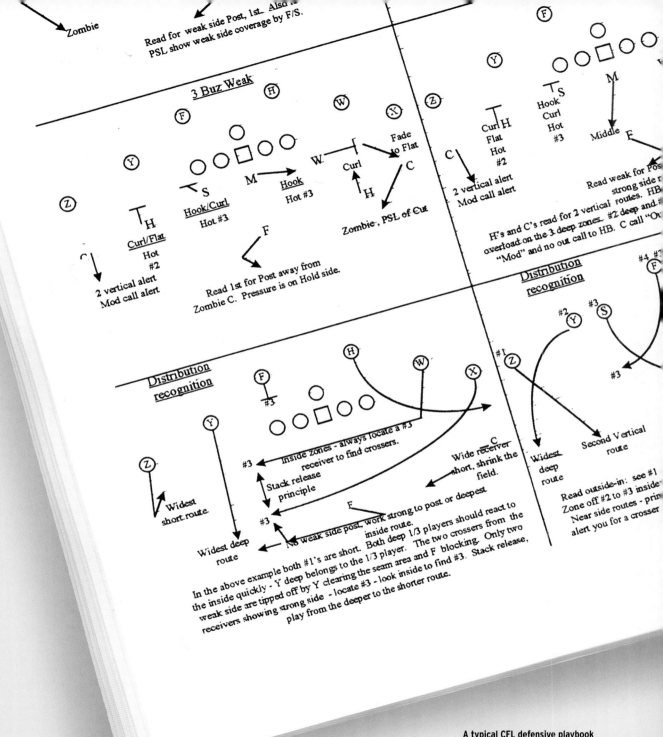

A typical CFL defensive playbook containing 150 pages of detailed adjustments.

IT'S OK TO BE SMART

"My high school football coach was my English teacher, and he created an environment on the football team where it was cool to be smart or knowledgeable," says Mike Clemons. "That was key for me. He encouraged me to not be afraid to seek out knowledge, to always ask questions, to study various aspect of the game. I learned early that football was not just a game of brute force, but also a mental game."

Mike O'Shea has become the undisputed leader of the Argos defence in recent years. He spends much of his time studying the big picture. "Football is a joy to me, all aspects, but I find it really intriguing to study good schemes," he says. "The best part is to see an offensive play unfold out there that you recognize, either from film work or past games, and are able to start your reaction prior to the play even being run. You can learn to make faster and better decisions, and that is probably my strongest asset right now."

Another facet of knowing the Big Picture is the importance of assessing the individual competition and considering how effective the player has been up to that point in the game. A defence may abandon the blitzing game (where the defensive backs are required to cover receivers one-on-one with no safety help), for example, because a receiver has just beaten a defensive back for a long touchdown. I have even been in huddles where a defensive back has begged the signal-caller not to use "zero coverage" (man-to-man with no safety help), because he knows the opposing wide receiver has his number and his confidence is shot.

As an offensive play begins to develop, the defensive players need to reflect on the Big Picture and use their past experiences to get an early read on the possible offensive intentions. Offences in the CFL routinely have as many as twenty different alignment possibilities. Adding to the difficulties for the defensive players are the motion rules in the CFL, which allow all but five players to be in motion prior to the snap. Defensive players must adjust their alignment in response to the movement patterns of the offensive players, so they can be in the most advantageous position when the play begins to unfold.

Elfrid Payton is one of the all-time best pass-rushers because of his ability to sack quarterbacks, a feat he has accomplished 154 times, only three short of Grover Covington's all-time CFL record of 157. His ability to read the play – factoring in numerous cues, including the splits of the offensive tackle opposite him, the alignment and motion of the backs and the cadence of the quarterback's signal-calling – is simply phenomenal. "My goal is to get to the quarterback," Payton says, "and my ability to get this done is because I know how offensive players play. I have developed my moves to take advantage of what I predict will happen next."

ABOVE O'Shea (left) displaying leadership on the field in typical fashion.

"*Football is a joy to me, all aspects, but I find it really intriguing to study good schemes.*"

– *Mike O'Shea*

Down for the Count

Seconds before a play is initiated, the offence is poised to begin the snap count. The players on the offensive team survey the defensive alignment and make their pre-snap moves. The quarterback reaches under the centre. His head turns slowly as he scans the defence. On the other side of the line of scrimmage, the defence jockeys with its alignments. Players crouch into their starting stance. Their muscles tense as they wait for the moment when the ball is snapped. These few seconds are a time of tension. The outcome of the game may be hanging in the balance.

This is what constitutes a down in football. This sequence of events is re-enacted sixty to eighty times a game. Each player has a job to do that has been stitched into memory through extensive repetition in both practice and games. When the ball is snapped, his responses need to be almost automatic.

The defensive team breaks the huddle and lines up before the offensive team does in order to study the offensive formation. As members of the defensive squad size up the opposition, each player mentally reviews his responsibilities, compares what he sees to his knowledge of the other team's offence and positions himself on the field accordingly. He may also take into account any number of other factors, including the score, field position, down and distance needed, the time on the clock and even who has an edge in play up to this point in the game. "You try to get a snapshot of the other team's intentions," explains O'Shea. "You search your brain to remember the types of plays they are likely to run out of the set they are in, and you anticipate the blocking scheme, all the movement patterns they are likely to use."

HUT ONE! HUT TWO!

The quarterback is the captain of the offence. He calls the intended play in the huddle, usually in the form of coded phrases. It may sound something like, "Zero – seventy-seven – fifty-four – stop on three." As the huddle breaks and the players assemble themselves in the designated formation, the quarterback surveys the defensive alignment, deciding whether his play selection is appropriate to what he sees. If not, he may choose to change the play at this time – to call an "audible" – using a word or phrase that the players recognize as code for a change. The next word he utters, usually a colour or a series of numbers, indicates the new play he has selected. Following this, he gives the offensive players a signal to prepare to move by barking out another code word, such as "blue," followed by the proverbial "hut one, hut two, hut three," or some other similar patter. On the designated number (which has been called in the huddle), the centre snaps (huts) the ball to the quarterback, and everyone is off and running.

> *"Come game day, anyone who had the other colour jersey on was the enemy, and they were all live game."*
>
> — Ben Zambiasi

Barron Miles plays defensive back as though he knows something no one else does. He is sneaky, sly and extremely smart. "The work you do in the film room, on the practice field and in communication with your teammates prepares you for accurate anticipation of offensive tendencies," he says. "Given the offensive formation, field position, down and distance information and early offensive motion, it is sometimes obvious what the offence is planning to run. There is so much information available before the snap that a good defender can get the jump on most offensives."

ABOVE The Lions' Barron Miles (9), showing uncharacteristic aggression, closes in on Saskatchewan's Corey Holmes (19).

OPPOSITE The Saskatchewan defence is very definitely at the right spot, stopping Hamilton's Troy Davis (middle) in his tracks.

WHAT HAPPENS NEXT

Former Montreal Alouettes head coach and longtime defence guru Rod Rust calls the brief period that follows the snap the "three-step phase." Rust suggests that in the time it takes the quarterback to take just three steps, almost all the information that the defensive squad requires is presented to them. During this phase, with the offensive team committed to running the play called in the huddle, all defensive players, no matter what position, are able to read the planned play. The better the player, the more accurate the prediction.

Alondra Johnson, with fifteen years' experience as a middle linebacker, explains the significance of small signs. "Most of the time I can recognize the play almost before it happens, not even using my thought processes too much. Just reacting on a hunch, a small clue or movement. The way a running back takes off, or the blocking pattern of the offensive guard — I just react to the movement. I don't have to be looking at

the wide receivers to notice them out of the corner of my eye. The blocking pattern of offensive players directly in front of me indicates that the play will go to the outside, and if you have played football long enough, you just know that an outside play is likely to have a wide receiver involved in a blocking angle that you better notice. I am not one of those guys who gets fooled a lot, gets cracked back on or pancaked."

Joe Fleming remembers an incident in the 2001 Grey Cup, when he was playing for Calgary. "I was pass-rushing on the play," he relates, "and I noticed Brett MacNeil, [Winnipeg's] offensive guard, take a quick look inside, and at that moment I knew I could make an inside move on the offensive tackle and come clean. I got to Khari Jones for an important sack in that game, because I knew that the guard, Brett, was not going to be able to help his tackle out when I took an inside route to the quarterback."

The Right Spot at the Right Time

If defensive players knew what the play was and where it would be run, it would be simple to shut it down. For example, if each player knew the offence was going to run a draw play into the interior of the line of scrimmage, the defensive linemen would pass-rush with less enthusiasm, the linebackers would not bother with their pass drops, and the defensive backs would be in no hurry to deploy into their pass defence. Instead, the defence would throw the running back for a loss and radio and television commentators would remark glowingly on the superior athletic skill of the player making the tackle.

But when the defence accurately anticipates an offensive play, athletic skill has little to do with the outcome; it is experience and perception that make the difference. The key to defensive success is to be in the right place at the right time.

The best defensive players understand the significance of every subtle shift in position, the adjustment of every alignment, the rearrangement of every movement pattern. They know where to look and what to watch for. They draw on what they have seen in practice situations, film study and prior plays. The confidence with which an individual plays likely correlates directly with the strength of his belief that he has accurately predicted the play.

EVERY MOMENT, EVERY MOVEMENT

After ten years in the CFL, mostly with the Calgary Stampeders, defensive back Marvin Coleman plays with a lot of confidence. "It is very important to know each receiver you face, to really understand his skills, his favourite moves and even his attitude," Coleman asserts. "Sometimes I feel as if I'm playing a mental game against the receiver, trying to hide what I know, trying to get him to do what I want him to do."

Each play is like a game in miniature. Each has its own planning and execution phases. There is always a pause between plays, from the time the referee blows his whistle to end one play, until the centre snaps the ball at the beginning of the next play. In this brief interval, the opposing teams have an opportunity to plot new strategy based on what they have learned from the previous trials. Those who can focus most effectively on the moment, who can select the most appropriate response from the vast repertoire of possible choices, are most likely to attain greatness.

It is neither athletic ability alone nor even luck that allowed Hall of Fame defensive back Less Browne to intercept eighty-seven balls over the course of his eleven-year career. He was able to make big plays

OPPOSITE, LEFT Defensive captain Reid enjoys the Alouettes' 2002 Grey Cup victory.

OPPOSITE, RIGHT As a defensive-back coach, Less Browne continues to use the mental skill he developed as a player.

LEFT Marvin Coleman is another example of a defensive player who understood the importance of mental preparation.

because he was able to put himself in the right place at the crucial moment. "Later in my career," he says, "I felt confident about knowing what was about to happen. I often tried to influence the play by lining up wrong and baiting the quarterback to throw to the receiver I was covering. I really felt that I could predict the play and had the confidence to act on my anticipation." In 1994, his last year in the CFL, Browne nabbed eleven interceptions and made a significant contribution to the B.C. Lions' Grey Cup win.

Every time they line up for another play, the defensive players' brains are going a mile a minute. Stefen Reid, who has been both an Ottawa Rough Rider and Montreal Alouette, was one of the most astute defensive players I ever encountered. Like Browne, he was an expert at using anticipation as a tool for success. "I am fascinated by the game as a whole, by deciphering the weakness in the opposing offensive system and in our own defensive plan. I love decoding the game. I'm in a mind-lock with the offensive coordinator. In fact, my biggest rush is knowing what play they are running before they run it."

Reid recalls an incident from a game in 1999 that shows how intently a defensive player concentrates on every aspect of the offensive team's pre-snap preparation. "We were playing Saskatchewan, and [Saskatchewan head coach] Danny Barrett was sending in the play with hand signals. I had been studying him and noticed a pattern throughout the first quarter. I had seen a similar pattern of signals from him in previous games through film study, and my suspicions were confirmed by the offensive plays they were running. You should have seen the faces of the some of the offensive players when I began shouting out their plays prior to the snap!"

Joe knows: You are not out there by yourself. You need to rely on your teammates to get the job done.

You Can't Do it Alone

There are no individual stars on winning defences. Every defensive player knows that without highly effective, coordinated team play, no player would be able to consistently shine. In fact, the ability to communicate, to play off of one another and to work as a unit are highly developed skills possessed by all great defensive players.

Defensive end Joe Montford argues, "Defensive players, especially the ones closest to your position, need to function as a unified team. The coach defines the defensive package, and you learn your responsibilities within this defensive scheme. It is understood that you need to be able to do the physical part – defeating the blocks in your gap, making the tackle when the ball carrier shows up in your area – the basic stuff of football, the stuff you have been conditioned to do since you first began playing. The mental part of the game – to be able to recognize what is happening and make the appropriate adjustment – defines when you really start to play well. For example," Montford continues, "my strengths are my quickness and my speed, especially in rushing the passer. In order to maximize my strengths, I need to be allowed to take chances, go a little on instinct. Sometimes, when I feel it is right, I will go inside the tackle to make a play even though you are taught in the defensive scheme that the defensive end is responsible for quarterback containment. [When I am] playing with an experienced teammate like Mike Philbrick, he recognizes when I leave my area of responsibility, and he covers for me, maybe sliding to the outside in case the quarterback breaks contain."

SIZE ISN'T EVERYTHING

Joe Montford says that stubborn pride had a lot to do with his growth as a player. "When we wanted to play basketball, we always got to the court early, and then the older kids would decide it was their turn and run us off. One day I decided I was going to stay on the court…. It probably was a bad decision, but I was determined – stubborn, I suppose. One of the biggest kids threatened me. There was a huge mud puddle at one end, and he dropped me on my head into that puddle. I remember to this day the feeling I had about wanting the chance to prove myself and the stubbornness I displayed."

Montford is a relatively small player at 225 pounds. He says, "There is a myth out there that you need to be a certain size to play a certain position or to play a certain way. Once I got the chance to participate, I could demonstrate that I was capable, and I was usually very good at whatever I did."

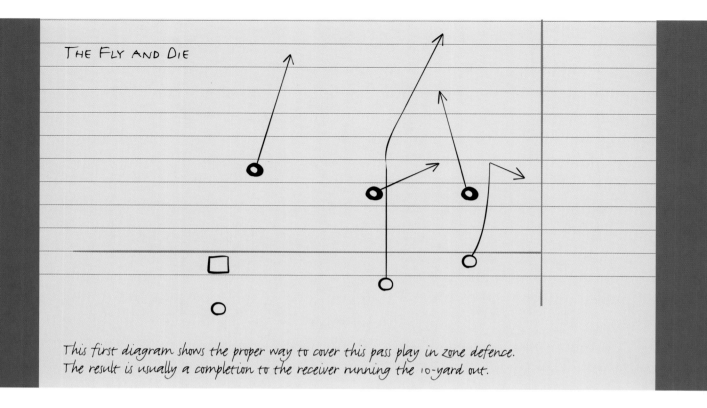

THE FLY AND DIE

This first diagram shows the proper way to cover this pass play in zone defence. The result is usually a completion to the receiver running the 10-yard out.

When Marvin Coleman was traded to the Winnipeg Blue Bombers in 2003, he immediately identified Harold Nash as a player like himself, with a similar understanding of the game. "We hit it off right away," Coleman recalls. "Communication is so much more than talking. It means understanding the position of the other player, understanding the problems he might face against each situation, like a combination route, for example." Coleman describes a play in which an implicit understanding is essential to effective defence. He talks about the route called "the fly and die," where the inside receiver runs up-field and breaks to the corner behind the cornerback. At the same time the outside receiver runs a ten- to twelve-yard out. "When you are playing a zone defence," Coleman explains, "there is no easy way to cover this pattern. If the corner does what he is supposed to and drops off to cover the deeper corner route, the quarterback just throws to the shorter out pattern. There is no way the defensive halfback can get to the out pattern on the sidelines from his position. Conversely, if the cornerback cheats

to take away the shorter out pattern, the deeper corner pattern will be open. Again, the defensive halfback can't turn and run with the corner route because he is supposed to be taking away the flat area. To make a long story short, Harold and I saw eye-to-eye on this dilemma. We had both played long enough that we understood each other's problem and knew almost instinctively what we needed to do." As soon as they recognized the route developing, Coleman says, both he and Nash reacted in a coordinated fashion. "I know that Harold is not going to let the inside receiver get an outside release on him," Coleman states. "This way he can funnel the inside receiver to the free safety, not letting him get to the corner easily. By trusting in Harold's correct read of this situation, I can take away the out pattern of the wide receiver. If you watched the film of how we play this pattern, you would think we were playing man-to-man coverage."

Joe Fleming had a similar rapport with Alondra Johnson in Calgary. "He knew exactly how defensive football worked," says Fleming. "On running plays,

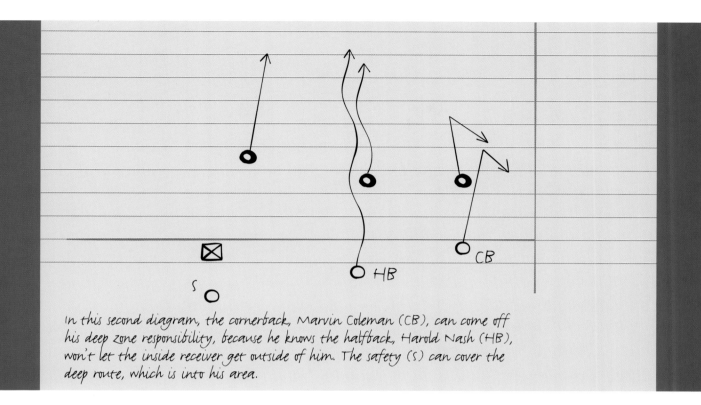

In this second diagram, the cornerback, Marvin Coleman (CB), can come off his deep zone responsibility, because he knows the halfback, Harold Nash (HB), won't let the inside receiver get outside of him. The safety (S) can cover the deep route, which is into his area.

I knew if I monopolized two blockers he would make the play. I felt it was my duty to keep him free of blockers. He completely understood this principle, and on blitzing plays he would often reciprocate. Rather than try to get to the quarterback by himself, he would often grab the offensive guard on the way by, thereby freeing me up for a run at the quarterback. Many of my sacks were in fact assisted by Alondra."

Gene Gaines argues that communication and teamwork are the keys to effective defensive play. "You end up playing over your weaknesses," he maintains, "often having another player overlapping your responsibilities, perhaps because he knows what stress you are under in a specific situation, and he knows that you need his help. This level of communication is only learned over time and is much more prevalent among great players. The network of understanding, of how you help each other, is what you are striving for as a coach and hopefully as a player. Great players will make plays, but a team-oriented player will win games."

Mike O'Shea also knows the importance of executing his responsibility and trusting his teammates to carry out their own. He describes the situation that develops when playing as a linebacker on a screen pass. "When I recognize there are two offensive linemen out in front of the receiver," he says, "I will try to split the two blockers, taking both of them out of further play. This manoeuvre is likely to get me eliminated from the play, but it allows another of my teammates to make an uncontested tackle." The player who makes the tackle will get the acclaim from the fans and media. He will also accumulate a statistic that will go on his record. Only his teammates and his coaches will know who really made the play by carrying out his responsibility within the specific defensive scheme.

"I really, really like the opportunity to hit people." – Alondra Johnson

ABOVE Calgary's defensive front hunkers down for a goal line stand.

OPPOSITE Vaughn's attitude on the football field has always been one of the hunter.

Attitude

Johnson was exactly right when he made his remark about "scaredy cats." Defensive football is a violent game requiring an aggressive, almost arrogant, attitude. "I really, really like the opportunity to hit people," he admits. "I suppose it's a good thing that I had football in my life. I don't know where I might have ended up without the opportunity to release my aggressive tendencies…. When I hit somebody just right, it is like I am having an orgasm, because it feels so good all over. I don't know if others feel that way. I suspect many do who wouldn't express it in those terms. The best part is that you are not tired after a good hit. You are ready for more. Sick, eh?"

Gerald Vaughn is widely known throughout the CFL as one of the very toughest defensive backs, a physical player who never backs down from a challenge. He represents a class of defensive back that displays all the characteristics of fundamental football.

When you take away the film work, the diagrams and the coaching schemes, football is basically a gladiatorial contest between testosterone-filled athletes. A smart and vicious player is a scary thing — and a coach's dream. "I love playing against tough receivers," enthuses Vaughn. "Not necessarily big, strong ones, but the ones who will do anything they need to [do to] make the catch. I get up close to the line of scrimmage where I can get a 'lick' on the receiver — try to intimidate him, you know, try to get him thinking about something other than his pass route or making the easy catch. The best receivers are the ones that you can't throw off their game. Even if you really punish them on a play, they are still capable of coming right back at you and making a difficult catch in traffic or throwing a 'pick' on you. Terry Vaughn and Ben Cahoon are two of the receivers that come to mind when I think of tough players.... When I'm playing against them I know I'm involved in a fight, and this

is one of the reasons I love to play football."

Rob Hitchcock patrolled Hamilton's defensive backfield for eleven years, intimidating receivers with his "no-quarter" style of play. "Football is a violent game, and physical domination is held in very high esteem," he points out. "I tried to establish a position that if you were going to come into my area, you had better be prepared to pay the price. Often a big hit on a receiver paid huge dividends — either the receiver would be more than likely to drop the next pass if they felt you were close, or it might inspire the rest of your teammates. I hit Tyree Davis of the Alouettes in 1999 with a knockout blow that left him unconscious on the field for a few minutes. That play totally energized the defensive, and we coasted to victory on that day."

Ben Zambiasi, another Hamilton player and one of the most feared linebackers to play in the CFL, explains just how seriously and personally he takes the game. "Many defensive players have a gladiatorial attitude on

the field. You are the enemy just because you are wearing the wrong-colour jersey. I was always committed to going after anyone on the other team: any running back, crossing receiver or even offensive lineman just standing around the pile. I would especially go after you if you were a dirty player or took cheap shots. I remember once, playing in the Eastern final against Winnipeg. Joe Poplawski, their slotback, hit me right in the back on a play [where] I was nowhere near the action. I took his number, and from then on I was looking for him. I found him later running a hook pattern, and I had a ten-yard run at him. Tom Clements, their quarterback at the time, told me after the game that Joe told him that it was the hardest hit he had ever taken and please not to throw any more balls to him for the rest of the game."

THE WILL TO WIN

Joe Montford's success is reflected in the level of arrogance he displays on the field. When you play defensive end in the CFL you are, on almost every play, in a one-on-one competition with the offensive tackle. When you regularly win those battles, you acquire something of a reputation, and Montford admits that his success has ended up being a motivating force for him. "At this point in my career, my challenge is to live up to my reputation," he says. "I have been successful, and the standard is very high. It is almost like I'm afraid to fail. There is a certain sense of paranoia, and it is a great motivator. One way I

set goals for myself is to understand that the offensive tackle has to be pretty much 100 per cent to have a great day. If he loses twice during the game, that's two sacks, and he is considered defeated by the defensive player. So I hope to beat my guy twice each game and, hopefully, both of those times the quarterback still has the football. In some sense it is about how long the quarterback holds the ball, but you win as a defensive lineman if he throws the ball away or makes a bad throw. Pressuring the quarterback to make mistakes is the name of the game."

When the will to win infects the entire defence you can become almost unstoppable. "I was playing for Calgary in the 2001 Western final up in Edmonton," Joe Fleming remembers. "We were supposed to get blown out, and early in the game we turned the ball over on our own one-yard line. The defence took to the field, and I could sense that the level of determination was special. On the first play, a quarterback sneak, we had about six of our defenders in their backfield causing mayhem. The ball came loose, we picked it up and that set the tone for the rest of the game. We went on to create, I think, nine turnovers and carried it over into the Grey Cup game the following week."

KNOWING YOURSELF, PLAYING WITHIN

Until you really know yourself, you are unlikely to maximize your potential. Your growth as a defensive football player will be held back by your inability to recognize your weaknesses and to make the necessary adjustments. It is relatively easy to play football on talent alone: just do what the coaches tell you to do, and let your athletic ability do the rest. At the CFL level, the problem is that all the other players are just as talented as you are. The factor that begins to separate great from good players is their ability to know themselves and to play within their abilities.

It didn't take Stefen Reid long to figure out that he needed to maximize his mental talents if he was to survive in the CFL. "I recognized early in my professional career that I wasn't the most physically talented athlete that we had on defence, and I knew that if I was to succeed, I would have to be a step ahead of the other guys, you know, a step ahead cerebrally. I had to be able to think things through and make quick plays mentally so that my body, my weaknesses and my physical attributes wouldn't hold me back. I think it is a matter of that balance between keeping healthy enough physically to be able to fulfill your role in the physical aspect of the defence and continue to gain experience, so that mentally you are improving. I spend a lot of time talking with our offensive coordinator, trying to understand the way that he looks at defences and the way that he would attack defences." Reid believes that this tactic helps him as a defensive player, and he cites it as an example of something that might give him an edge over other players.

WHAT IS IT?

POWER-RUSH
Defensive linemen use this term to describe their attempt to overpower a blocker by pushing him backward on the way to rushing the quarterback.

DOWN-BLOCK
A technique in which the offensive tackle tries to contact a defensive player who is aligned closer to the offensive centre.

DRIVE-BLOCK
An attempt by offensive linemen to attack aggressively and push the defender backward.

PICK
A manoeuvre whereby one offensive receiver "accidentally" runs into a defensive player who is the process of covering another receiver.

Alouettes linebacker Reid is constantly calculating, constantly making decisions.

"I knew that if I was to succeed, I would have to be a step ahead of the other guys…a step ahead cerebrally." – Stefen Reid

Elfrid Payton's expertise as a football player is in his ability to rush the passer. Knowing both himself and his opponent has allowed him to stay at the top of his game. "I have always been a pass-rusher," he says, "whether from the defensive line position or from linebacker, since I was in high school. I was always smaller than my opponent. I was always quick, but I had to develop good technique if I was to survive playing defensive line. I know body language and can use it to get clues from the offensive tackles. I know when he is going to use a down-block, set up to pass-block or drive-block me before he does it. It is child's play. On runs, when the tackle plans to drive-block me, I know I need to crash down inside, cause a pile, because I am not big enough to take on his block. Or when a tackle steps inside, my eyes go right to the ball. I know it is going to be a shovel pass or a counter play. I am not afraid to gamble more than other defensive players. I know what I can do, and usually I am right. I feel that it is the offensive players and coaches that need to study me and worry about how they will prepare to play against me. I try not to let coaches or other players influence me too much. I use the instincts from fourteen years in this league to play my own game."

This level of arrogance, while not usually characterized as such by other defensive players, is typical of the attitude needed to be a successful CFL defender. Payton knows his own strengths (his speed, agility and quick hands) and his weaknesses (his relative lack of strength and size), and he understands how to minimize the latter while exploiting the former.

"All my play is instinctive. I never watch film, I do not study my opponents and could care less about what the other team is trying to do."

– Elfrid Payton

With 154 career quarterback sacks, Payton was an offensive tackle's challenge and a quarterback's nightmare.

Barron Miles floats though the air to break up a pass intended for a Renegade receiver.

Barron Miles' skill and proficiency are impressive. His style of play is so effortless, so controlled and so different from my own desperate, insecure style. He acknowledges his own limitations and yet appears to have total confidence in his abilities and has clearly found a way to master his role. "I am a little too quiet for modern-day football," he concedes. "I am not loud-mouthed or flamboyant. I am more studious, disciplined and can play with finesse. I try to keep an even keel. I certainly don't consider myself the smartest player, but I am aware of what I know and what I don't know. I try to not let my ego limit my understanding of how to play effectively. I think many players don't know themselves well enough.... We watch film almost every day and I see players continually making dumb mistakes – many times because of their egos – or misreading a play as it is developing. I try to not to be arrogant about my abilities. In fact, I have learned not to be, because the moment you relax and take something for granted is when you are most vulnerable. The other team's receivers are working to better their game and you need to have a healthy level of respect for them. Ideally, I like to get the sense that I am playing scared without being scared. I suppose it is a heightened sense of awareness."

"I am fast enough, quick enough and athletic enough for any opponent; it is the mental game that I must concentrate on to be successful. If you relax even for one play, that's when you are going to get beaten." – Barron Miles

I was happy for Mike O'Shea that the Toronto Argonauts won the 2004 Grey Cup. To me, he was the heart and soul of that team, a team that struggled offensively throughout the 2004 season. Damon Allen was hurt for much of the season and performed poorly when he did play. It was the Argo defence that kept the team in most games. They showed a lot of stubborn pride. The defensive unit has the power at times to rise above the rest of a team's deficiencies and decide that they are not going to lose. I have played on teams with that type of character. Besides his obvious qualities as a player, O'Shea is also a thoughtful, balanced individual, more at home talking about schemes, team play and concentration than about his personal accomplishments. He acknowledges that, after twelve years in the league, his physical abilities have dropped off and he has had to learn to compensate. "Now, more than ever," he says, "I'm into the concept of effective team play, and I can always improve in this area. I love this about football, the sense that you control much of what happens based on your own and your teammates' preparation and attitude. This is what is called teamwork. You have so many opportunities to make a difference. There are so many plays. You always seem to have another chance."

6

Mostly a Mental Game

No business could survive if it were run the way the kicking game is run in the CFL. It is astonishing that more resources are not allocated to this aspect of the game. The outcome of countless contests rides on the kicker, but not a single CFL team currently has a full-time kicking coach. In fact, to the best of my knowledge, no CFL team has ever had one. Occasionally a team might bring in a former kicker to work with a player who is struggling. Or they might send a kicker to a kicking camp for a few days. All teams assign responsibility for managing the kicking teams to an assistant coach, but this job does not involve actually coaching the kicker.

Paul McCallum endures his worst nightmare: missing a kick on the last play that would have put his Roughriders in the 2004 Grey Cup final.

The moment of truth: Paul McCallum (right) swings toward the impact point.

**Mark McLoughlin (13) zones out
the turmoil, focusing solely on
"good contact."**

The kick-off, kick-off return, punt, punt-return, field goal, field-goal defence and touchdown conversion together make up approximately twenty-five to thirty per cent of the plays in any one game. The kicking teams score the majority of points earned in any football game. Lui Passaglia, the legendary kicker for the B.C. Lions, was responsible for 3,991 points during his twenty-five regular seasons. That total would represent 665 touchdowns, which is 391 more touchdowns than both George Reed and Mike Pringle scored during their combined twenty-six years in the league.

The kicker is the player who punts, does kick-offs, converts touchdowns and kicks field goals. The major distinction in skill sets is between punting and the more generic role of place-kicking. Some teams have two kickers, one each for the two types of kicking responsibilities. In Winnipeg, for example, Bob Cameron (1980–2002) handled the punting duties for twenty-three years; Troy Westwood (1991–2004) was responsible for all other kicking duties for twelve of those years. Passaglia, however, represented the more common arrangement, as he did almost all the kicking for the B.C. Lions for twenty-five years.

Just Close Your Eyes and Hope

Paul Osbaldiston, who handled the punting and kicking duties for the Hamilton Tiger-Cats for eighteen years, admits that he was pretty much left on his own to figure it out. "There has never been anyone out there to help me. I'm just the guy over there, the body that gets called out to the field periodically to perform. I think the coaches, by and large, just close their eyes and hope. It's up to me entirely to do whatever is necessary to get ready to do the job on the field."

Asked if he had ever had a kicking coach to give him feedback on his play, Passaglia says, "Nope." Did he ever ask a coach to watch him? "Nope." Did he have other kickers in camp to talk with? "Nope." Did he go to kicking camp? "Nope," he says and adds, "I learned predominantly by watching other kickers on TV, on film and across the league. The only time I ever had kickers to learn from was that first training camp, when we had kickers Eddie Murray and Eddie Thomas [two veterans who had NFL experience], when they were looking for that one kicker. Don't get me wrong; I wasn't arrogant about my abilities. I was a young, insecure Canadian like the rest of them. I worked hard at getting better. It was that I was left pretty much all on my own to do it. I copied other kickers. I even tried to kick straight away. I tied a string around my boot just like I had seen Dave Cutler [Edmonton Eskimos Hall of Fame kicker, 1969–84] do it in Edmonton. Literally, I tried everything I could think of."

Terry Baker played seventeen years in the CFL (1987–2002), but it wasn't until his fifteenth year that he received outside coaching. And he didn't get an on-field coach – he got a video. "Before the 2001 season, I helped a kicker from Mount Allison University, and he lent me a tape from the Dallas Cowboys' kicking coach. It was awesome. I changed my whole approach to practicing kicking. I worked back from the contact point. It got me more focused, and I ended up with a much more consistent approach to kicking. One game we played B.C. here in Montreal in a driving rainstorm. On one long field-goal attempt, the snap-back was low, and Ben Cahoon took extra time in getting it onto the tee. By that time I had taken my steps and lost any hope of momentum and leg drive. I just waited patiently until Ben had it right, and I kicked it with just my right leg swing. Boom! It went forty-seven yards into the teeth of a strong wind, squarely between the uprights. I totally believe I made that difficult kick because of the mechanical way I had prepared."

The Life of a CFL Kicker

Football practices can be pretty boring for the kicker. A typical practice is approximately two hours long, and the kicker interacts with other members of the team for a total of about fifteen minutes. Apart from a specific segment devoted to one of the kicking teams, he is off by himself, wandering around the periphery of the field. With no coach, the kicker learns to fill the time with drills of his own devising. "Often my biggest help on the team were the equipment managers and ball boys, shagging punts and place-kicks along the sidelines," says Baker.

Self-regulation is a central aspect of the CFL kicker's professional career. "I remember clearly one of the specific strategies I used way back when I first started my career," Passaglia relates. "Cal Murphy – now a Hall of Fame member – one of the assistant coaches and not a kicking coach at all, suggested that I use the white lines across the field to kick along. This small piece of advice has been a significant factor for me. I still use it to check on the swing of my leg and the path of the ball."

Osbaldiston remembers a difficult period early in his career when he struggled with his solitary role. "The first few years that I played in the league were unbelievable for me. What a difficult learning process I went through! I look back and I wonder how I was successful at all, at any time. On every missed kick or error of execution I was filled with self-doubt and had no one to guide or console me. Then I found there was a middle section of my career when I was discovering what was going on, learning a lot more and applying what I was learning. This part can be categorized as more comfortable, trying things, experimenting, not so intimidated by the whole atmosphere. It made the whole idea of kicking in the CFL a whole lot easier, more relaxed. For the last eight to ten years, given the experience I have, each kick is evaluated and categorized, enabling me to put everything into perspective. Everything seems so clear to me now. I always know why a kick was successful or what factor affected the outcome. I have learned to be self-critical, using the framework of past experiences to analyze my kicks and to monitor my own performance."

"Mental imagery is a key tool for kickers. I always walk along both hash marks both ways prior to the game, and while I'm doing this I talk to myself about particular things I've reminded myself about." – Paul Osbaldiston

Terry Baker – alone with his craft, alone with his thoughts.

The Moment of Truth

The most critical play in many football games occurs during the dying seconds, and it's often a field-goal attempt. The last kick of Passaglia's career was a game-winning field goal in the 2000 Grey Cup game. And in 1994 his last-second field goal enabled the B.C. Lions to defeat the Baltimore Stallions 26–23 to win the Grey Cup.

Given the pressure they have to endure, it's easy to understand why field-goal kickers often trot slowly onto the field. Generally they don't even go into the offensive huddle. They are in their own world, going through a pre-kick phase of mental preparation. Passaglia says, "I learned a long time ago that once you cross over that white sideline you need to be in the zone. The best example I can remember was in the 1994 Grey Cup game: last-play field goal to win the game. [When I looked] at the game film later, my actions were incredibly revealing to me. I don't remember much about the play, my feelings or thought process at the time. I just ran off the bench to the exact spot, placed the tee down, took a deep breath and kicked the ball dead centre through the posts. You have to learn to focus when it's your time. All good kickers have routines they use to establish that moment of understanding. Dave Cutler used to jog out across the thirty-five-yard line before his field-goal attempts, regardless of where the field goal was to be kicked from. We become creatures of habit, learning to prepare ourselves in consistent, comfortable ways."

*"You have to learn to
focus when it's your time."*

– Lui Passaglia

**ABOVE Kicking the 2000 Grey
Cup-winning field goal in his last game,
after twenty-five years of football,
certainly is a dramatic statement for
the Lions' Passaglia (5).**

**LEFT Surrounded by his teammates,
Passaglia celebrates the Lions' 1994
Grey Cup win — also the result of a
game-winning field goal by this
formidable kicker.**

Field goals are both the most precise of the
kicking-game challenges and the most complex. There's
precious little time to think about it. Figure 0.7 seconds
for the snap, 0.5 seconds for the holder to place the
ball on the tee and 1.2 seconds for the kicker to
complete his approach. If the kicker takes any longer
than that, the chances of having the ball blocked go
way up. The likelihood of the kick being blocked is fifty
per cent if the kicker's run-up takes as much as 1.5
seconds. (Longer attempts are also more likely to be
blocked because the kick requires less loft to get the
added distance.) The difference between 1.2 and 1.5
seconds is mighty fine, especially considering that you
have to factor in the contribution of not just one, but
three individuals. All three have to perform their tasks
impeccably in this time frame. Quite a level of precision
combined with a very high level of trust among the
participants.

Osbaldiston observes that once you've been in
the league for a number of years, the kicker's task is
mostly mental. "You have confidence in your technique
and know your range," he says, but you have to
"prepare yourself for each kick. Before the game I'll
use mental imagery, picturing the ball going through
the uprights, imagining the effect of the wind on the
ball while standing at certain points on the field. During
the pre-game warm-up, I always walk down both hash
marks both ways. While doing this I talk to myself about
particular things I've reminded myself about. As I line
up for a kick I go through a very specific process that
hasn't varied in years. I could recite it in my sleep. I use

Eskimos legend Dave Cutler (right) kicks the game-winner in the 1981 Grey Cup against Ottawa.

"Kicking in the CFL is a lot less precise than in the NFL, and that puts added pressure on the kickers. We are often expected to make it up as we go along, adapt to the inconsistencies."

– Lui Passaglia

the goal post as an alignment orientation with respect to the angle of my approach. I speak to myself as I prepare to kick, reminding myself to keep my body speed down and upper body over the ball and then having an inside-out leg swing. I never think about the other players when I'm kicking."

Passaglia suggests that most field goal kickers practice too much, kick too many balls, in each session. "During my last year – and remember that was twenty-five years down the road – I kicked less during the year than I ever did before. I made forty out of forty-four field goals that year, including a forty-nine-yard game-winning kick in Montreal. That year I had the best kicking percentage I ever had, and to top it all off I made the game-winning field goal in the last game I ever played in: the 2000 Grey Cup." But, with a knowing grin on his face, he acknowledges that it took him twenty-four years of kicking to get to the point where he could be confident in deciding to practice kicking less often. Small solace for young, aspiring field-goal kickers.

It's not easy being a kicker. Noel Prefontaine (1) takes some bone-crunching abuse.

Terry Baker (10) shows good concentration, though his punt is blocked by a lunging Renegade.

More than Just Hang Time

It seems like such simple action: the ball comes back to the punter, and he just kicks it high and far. End of story. According to the men who are responsible for this task, it is so much more than that. "The defensive alignment, the location of the punt-returner, the position of the ball on the field, the weather conditions and even the location of a known punt-blocker are all variables that the punter needs to account for," maintains Osbaldiston. "For example, when we play Ottawa, I need to know where Gerald Vaughn is and where the punt-block attempt might be coming from. I can figure out if I need to be faster or change my punting angles."

"The wind is always a big factor, and how you punt, and even the direction you end up punting the ball, need to be factored in," explains Passaglia. "Kicking from one hash mark across the field to get the ball to go out of bounds is a high-risk venture, but if the wind is blowing across the field, it is probably your only option. If you miss, and the ball doesn't go out of bounds, you have put the coverage team at risk

because of the coverage angles and the potential of a big return. I am ultimately responsible to make the right decision and get the best punt off, considering the circumstances. I usually do not make the decisions on my own. The coaches tell me what they want me to do most of the time, but I am frequently asked for my input in less obvious situations. If you take off and run the ball because you thought you saw an opening, you had better be right."

Passaglia believes other factors have come into play recently, making the punter's job more difficult and less predictable. "In the last fifteen years, the kicker's job has changed somewhat," he comments. "With the improvements in kick returns, with many teams having kick-return specialists, teams spend more time on their return system. People have woken up to the size of the field. Kickers are now expected to read the returner, kick the ball away from him. Kicking it thirty-five yards out of bounds is better than kicking it fifty yards down the middle of the field."

Keith Stokes makes life miserable for the Lions' kicker and coverage team by returning this kickoff for a 90-plus-yard touchdown.

THE SPECIALIST

Each team now seems to have one designated kick-returner – a player who does not have any other primary position to learn. This is a relatively new phenomenon that has arisen over the past five to eight years. The basic idea is that the specialist will be fresh when sent out to retrieve the punt, kick-off or missed field-goal attempt. He will also be more focused on the task at hand, because he has not been preoccupied with the tasks required at another position.

It also seems that coaches are more likely to ask the specialist to return punts or missed field goals from their own end zones – traditionally something that coaches have been reluctant to do. In recent years it seems that missed field goal and long field goals attempts are, in reality, offensive plays. There has been a steady increase in returns of over forty yards and quite a few length-of-the-field touchdown scampers, usually considered a turning point of the game.

Head down, eyes on the ball and just
swing through; Sean Fleming (left)
executes to perfection.

"I'll tell you," Passaglia continues, "a kicker's ego has cost his team many a long punt return. I myself have been guilty on many occasions of trying to boom my best kick and consequently out-kicking the coverage team. Sometimes I would have to make touchdown-saving tackles on the returners, and the feeling I left the field with was not satisfaction on being able to bring the ball-carrier down, but embarrassment or anger at myself for not kicking more effectively. The Gizmo [Henry Williams, Edmonton Eskimos, 1986–2000] beat up our punt-coverage team on more than one occasion because of me."

WHAT IS IT?

POOCHED KICK
The kicker attempts to kick the ball high but not too far, allowing his teammates to get down the field before the defensive team has a chance to assume a blocking formation.

Henry "The Gizmo" Williams, Edmonton's kick returner *par excellence*, out-legging the pursuit — something he did for fifteen glorious years.

Passaglia probably passed and ran from the punter position more than any other kicker. He always thought he could have been a receiver in the league and practiced in that position for his first three years. It was Vic Rapp, the head coach of the B.C. Lions from 1979 to 1982, who finally told him he was never going to get on the field as a receiver. Still, Passaglia always felt he could contribute as an offensive weapon from the punting position. He found someone who appreciated what he could do when Don Matthews took on the head coaching responsibilities from 1983 to 1987. "His first year here in 1983," remembers Passaglia, "in the very first game he coached for us, on the first punting play, he lined our speedy wide receiver, Mervyn Fernandez, near the sideline even with me as the punter. I kicked a pooched line-drive punt about twenty-five or thirty yards down the field towards his side. He caught it on the first bounce and was away to the races. I loved the fact that Don Matthews designed all sorts of special plays for me. Another time, the ball was snapped to me in punt formation, and I got a sense that all the defensive players were tied up trying to block our cover guys. I just sort of took off with the ball straight up the field following the pack. No one noticed me. I had the ball out in front prepared to punt it on the run, but I just kept on going and going, just like that Energizer bunny. I think I made forty-five yards, and the player who finally caught me was the punt-returner. He was the only one who could see me with the ball."

*"Probably the most
important part of blocking
kicks is keeping your eyes
open the whole time."*
— Gerald Vaughn

Textbook form from Vaughn (39): eyes open, hands together, arms extended and a full-body layout in front of kicker Noel Prefontaine's foot.

A Specialized Skill

Gerald Vaughn has blocked twelve kicks in his CFL career, and Barron Miles and Less Browne have blocked eight. These players represent the apex of the kick-blocking fraternity. It is a very specialized skill that combines quickness, agility, concentration, instinct and nerve.

Vaughn regards punt-blocking, at least partly, as a technical skill. He breaks it down into elements – positioning, jumping, using hands – that can be practiced and taught. "I was always good at blocking kicks," he says, "as far back as high school. I really started to get good at it, though, at Ole Miss [the University of Mississippi] with focused coaching. Also, they started to develop schemes for me, so I got lots

of opportunities. The trick is to watch the ball, get a good take-off, have good leverage when getting by the blocker and know how to use your hands. Probably the most important part of blocking kicks is keeping your eyes open the whole time. This helps your concentration and helps you avoid contacting the kicker."

Miles talks less about the technique than about attitude. "With success comes confidence, and now I believe I can block almost every kick. It's about attitude, and this is one area of football that I am cocky about. My attitude sets me apart from many others. I wish the coaches would allow me an opportunity to try more blocks, even on my own. I am sure I would be successful more often than not."

Vaughn knows how to block kicks and loves the challenge of doing so.

7

Great Players, Great Teams

Do players become great by playing on teams that win, or do teams that win have great players? Are great teams composed of individuals who buy into a team philosophy, or are they made up of a group of great individual players? Most coaches and players recognize that they need a certain level of physical talent. They can't do without some gifted players who have the potential to be great. But they will also tell you that they need players with character who commit to working together to achieve shared goals. They know that the best players are singularly driven to succeed. But they also know that the great ones understand the only way to succeed in football is to play effectively with their teammates. Much of their focused effort goes into learning to work with coaches and teammates to refine their play and understand their role in the team structure.

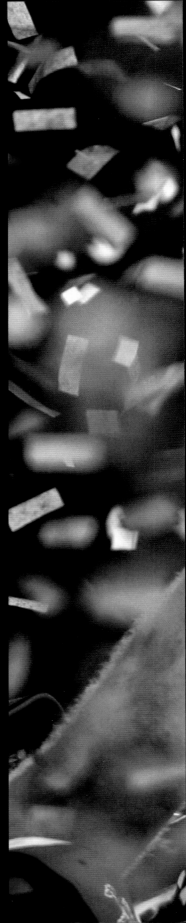

The holy grail of Canadian football: every player's dream, and the greatest players' quest.

Individual Commitment and Team Play

In this age of media-hyped personalities, of egocentric athletes and of vast differences in salary among teammates, it is not easy to build the cohesion and trust required to bind a team together. Coaches, general managers and scouts try to bring to training camp players they think will solve the teamwork puzzle.

It is easy to recognize a gifted athlete. He is the one with speed, size, agility and the ability to execute football skills at a consistently high level. You see lots of these athletes at every training camp. I thought almost every defensive back the Alouettes brought in to compete for my job throughout my twelve years in the CFL was a better athlete than I was. I played and thrived in the league not because of my athletic superiority, but because I learned to minimize my mistakes, understand my role in the defence and play effectively with my teammates.

Marv Levy says, "Greatness is about having a high level of performance over an extended period of time. It has a consistency to it." I believe that all the great players make a commitment to the game. They work hard to improve their play and in doing so develop a level of trust in their teammates that translates into superior individual and team success. No group of individuals worked harder, longer and with a stronger sense of purpose in this regard than the Edmonton Eskimos from 1974 to 1982.

The Eskimos hoist head coach Hugh Campbell in the air upon winning their fifth Grey Cup in a row in 1982. This was a dynasty like no other.

During this nine-year period, the Eskimos made it to the Grey Cup final an astounding eight times. They won six of those eight games, including the last five in a row. It is reasonable to suppose that those Edmonton teams had their share of phenomenal athletes, the gems that general managers and scouts spend their careers trying to uncover. As a member of an opposing team during this period of Eskimo dominance, my perspective may be skewed, but it appears to me that only their quarterback Warren Moon and perhaps linebacker Dan Kepley merit recognition for individual brilliance. Rather than benefiting from the genius of a handful of standout players, it seems to me, Edmonton achieved its dynastic status in those years because all the players completely bought into the team idea.

"The coach's role is to be able to get the players to have the same picture in their heads as you have in yours. When they buy into or fully understand what you want them to do, you have laid the foundation of a winning team."

— Wally Buono

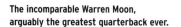

Rather than benefiting from the genius of a handful of standout players, it seems to me, Edmonton achieved its dynastic status in those years because all those players completely bought into the team idea.

Of the twenty-three Edmonton Eskimos in the CFL Hall of Fame, eleven of them played during that amazing nine-year stretch. Their Hall of Fame status has to owe a lot to the team's success. Their coach at the time, Hugh Campbell, certainly emphasizes the importance of their relationships to one another. "I feel that there are three types of players," he says. "The ones with good work ethic, strong personality and high skill levels that most fans and football people recognize as stars. Then there will always be a group of players who have gotten to this level on talent alone but lack the dedication and commitment to work hard. Thirdly, there are those in the middle, having talent and some aspect of good character traits. To have a good team, you need the leadership of the first group to influence the other two groups to come together with a common purpose. You can't coach everything, but I feel it is an important function of coaching to choose players who know what it takes to win, perhaps low-maintenance individuals who will do more than their responsibilities, who accept a lesser leadership role and create an environment where winning is actively pursued."

Campbell goes on to talk about some of the Edmonton players who didn't get the headlines in those days, "like Tom Towns, Dale Potter, Angelo Santucci and Don Warrington; players who would rather make the block to spring a Jim Germany or Warren Moon. They took pride in their accomplishments, knowing that their peers and coaches recognized the work they did, that it was an important component of a winning effort.

"In a similar vein," relates Campbell, "Waddell Smith, our starting wide receiver from those years, made a play that stands out in my mind, even after all these years. There was an interception on the play...and Waddell Smith ran the length of the field to catch the ball carrier on the five-yard line. We subsequently stopped them. [Saskatchewan] got no points, and I believe we went on to win the game. I showed that film over and over again to make the point: effort is a defining component of great teams. Waddell made a great play. That type of effort was infectious around the team when we won those five Grey Cups. Dan Kepley, a great middle linebacker, made that type of play almost every play. He epitomized the effort we expected our players to have. I suppose it is one of the main reasons he is in the Canadian Football Hall of Fame today."

Many knowledgeable players and coaches – not just Hugh Campbell – regard commitment to the team as paramount in establishing a winning attitude. Argo defensive captain Mike O'Shea says, "A big part of our team success in winning the Grey Cup in 2004, and one aspect that helps define a great player for me, is the ability of that player to make players around him better. In doing so, he makes it easier for everybody to come to work. I suppose I am talking about great leaders and, to make a point, Wayne Gretzky comes to mind. He had a way of making everyone better."

O'Shea also talks about the ideal relationship among teammates reflecting "a level of care," meaning a shared commitment and an unwillingness to let one another down. "Our defensive team in 2004 seemed to rise to this level of caring," he points out.

The last word here goes to Ron Lancaster: "Team chemistry is the key; I always say this. A player can bullshit the fans, he can bullshit the media and for a while he can get the coaches, but the people he can never bullshit are the guys in the locker room. They know. They know whether you are pulling your load. They know whether they can count on you when it gets tough. They know whether you're going to be ready to go every day."

"A player can bullshit the fans, he can bullshit the media and for a while he can get the coaches, but the people he can never bullshit are the guys in the locker room." – Ron Lancaster

Damon Allen (9) and Mike O'Shea celebrate after winning the 2004 Grey Cup.

"Some players naturally take over leadership roles....
Coaches have to allow that to happen if they expect
to have a winning team." – Marv Levy

Setting an Example

The commitment players make to their teammates is an essential component of successful leadership, and all great players have a leadership role on the team. They understand and accept that they are accountable both to themselves and to their teammates. Great players accept this responsibility. Marv Levy says, "Leadership does not come from the coaching staff. If you think you are doing that as a coach, the players are not necessarily on your side. Some players naturally take over leadership roles and you can see it happening on your team. The best ones do it at the right time and in the right way. Leadership is the ability to get other people to get the best out of themselves, and there are players who do that to their teammates.... Coaches have to allow that to happen if they expect to have a winning team. [The players] need to have the confidence to make difficult, spur-of-the-moment decisions, and the ones who do it best are what I call your team leaders."

There are many dedicated, committed players on every team in the CFL. Coaches can help establish an environment in which these players are allowed to emerge as leaders. As this develops, the best players take their responsibilities more seriously and, because they are accountable to the entire team, work harder to achieve team success.

A Locker-room Uprising

The Montreal Alouettes demolished the Edmonton Eskimos 41-6 in the 1977 Grey Cup. The next year, Marv Levy accepted a job as head coach of the NFL's Kansas City Chiefs and took some of his staff with him. Hence, the Alouettes began 1978 with an almost entirely new coaching staff. Joe Scannella replaced Levy as head coach, and he brought in Lamar Leachman to be the defensive coordinator along with incumbent Gene Gaines. Naturally the new crew attempted to install a new defensive playbook during training camp – but this is where the story takes an unexpected turn.

The players – and I was one of them – refused to accept the change.

Eight of the defensive starters had been with the Alouettes since 1972. They had been a major part of the team's success, including two Grey Cup wins. Most of the players wanted to continue with the system that they knew and in which they had confidence. Further, they wanted to be part of the development of the defensive game plan. An agreement was reached between the players, Leachman and Gaines to keep the familiar system, and the two coaches would work with the players to develop the defensive game plans. But the agreement had to be kept secret from Scannella, who had specifically forbidden this arrangement.

Gaines had been a player for sixteen seasons and our defensive-backs coach for the previous six years. He recognized the commitment and pride our particular group of players embodied. He believed in us enough that he was willing to transfer much of the responsibility for the fate of the defence to the players. In this way, we players made ourselves more accountable than any other group of players in professional football.

Our defence thrived in this environment. The defensive corps studied more film, held longer team meetings and even stayed after practice to work on fitness. We players made all the defensive calls in the games. We sent the signals back to the sideline to the two coaches, keeping them informed just in case Scannella asked what defence we were playing. This went on for two years, and the successful defence was a major factor in the Alouettes' participation in the following two Grey Cups. Wally Buono, current head coach of the B.C. Lions and one of the leaders of the Alouettes defences of the 1970s, has told me on occasion that duplicating that situation is one of the constant objectives he has as a coach. He believes "if you can get that level of commitment and leadership from the majority of your players, they will undoubtedly be better players for it."

Ron Estay is currently a defensive coach with Saskatchewan and was formerly a team leader with the great Eskimos teams of the late 1970s and early 1980s. He also recognizes that the players are the ones who need to understand the other teams' strategies and game plans to be effective. "You know, you have got to love what you are doing, and I think that is one reason why we were so successful. We were not only players, but also we were coaches. We could make adjustments on the field because we looked at and studied game film, discussed strategies with each other, and we did the same type of thing the coaches did. The whole defence would get in the film room before games and work together to really understand the opponent."

"I want guys on my team that practice to win, not just practice to play. They need to show me a level of intensity, of aggressiveness, an attitude that they are working to get better." – Ron Estay

Leadership on the Field

As many successful teams do, the current Montreal Alouettes team continues to involve the players in making defensive strategy. Bryan Chiu talks about his relationship with the coaching staff and his teammates. "Often I take a leadership role in team meetings, but I have to give coach Doug Berry [Alouette offensive coordinator, 1999–2005] a lot of the credit for our success. He is knowledgeable, but more importantly he understands offensive linemen, our needs, our personalities. He allows us to grow by involving us in all discussions, and even decision-making, when it comes to game planning. He doesn't tell us specifically what to do. He might say we need to block so-and-so and then ask us what is the best way to get the job done. It may be slower, more frustrating, dealing with various opinions, but by doing it this way we get to better understand each player's issues, sometimes even their insecurities. This process allows us to develop schemes that work to our strength.... This also forces us to accept the responsibility for the success of the scheme or play. If we fail, then we have to be accountable for the outcome."

The 2005 Calgary Stampeders, like all teams, have the potential to be great, but there is no set formula for success. It takes various forms of leadership to develop the necessary chemistry.

Bruce Beaton provides another example of how leadership often comes from the players themselves. "I was playing in Montreal in 1997 on a fabulous offensive line, blocking for Mike Pringle," he relates. "A problem began to emerge with one player not really pulling his weight to the satisfaction of the group.... One practice day we were running inside running plays, tuning up our timing, when Mike decided to show his style of leadership. He took the ball deep in the backfield and flat ran over the lineman. It didn't take any words for this player to get the message, and from then on he took a much more professional approach to his practice sessions."

The most effective leadership is often demonstrated through actions rather than words. Chiu took direct action to remind both an opponent and his teammates of their responsibilities to one another. "We were playing Toronto," Chiu recalls, "and Mike O'Shea took what I saw as a cheap shot on our quarterback, Anthony Calvillo. On the very next play I went straight for Mike and really roughed him up, possibly even a little over the edge, according to the rules. I felt I needed to send a message not only to Mike and the Argos, but also to our own teammates who, when reviewing the game film the following day, would recognize the play for what it is: a statement about the position on touching our quarterback."

Action is one thing; attitude is another. Joe Fleming says that Alondra Johnson assumed a leadership role with his team simply by the power of his presence. "I remember clearly," says Fleming, "in defensive huddles in Calgary, the look on [Johnson's] face was enough. The focused determination, the 'you will not beat me' attitude, was enough to inspire his teammates."

Estay recounts a story about Edmonton quarterback Tom Wilkinson. "Wilky never let up," he says. "One game we were beating Toronto 54-0. I was standing next to Hugh Campbell, our coach at the time, and he was agitated, squawking at Wilky, yelling, 'No! No!' Wilky wanted to continue to throw the ball, you know, run up the score. He wanted to beat you as bad as he could. I love that story, just the competitive nature of our game and about getting after [the other team]."

The Importance of Working Together

Each player has a specific set of responsibilities that he must both understand and execute flawlessly. Defensive linemen, for example, must be able to stop the run and rush the quarterback. Linebackers, the most versatile of the defensive groups, are asked to take on blocking linemen, be effective tacklers and cover backs on pass routes. Defensive backs have the demanding responsibility of covering fleet and elusive receivers across the vast Canadian field. In fact, all players are skilled in a multitude of tasks. And they all depend upon one another to do their jobs properly. There was not one of the forty-or-so CFL players I interviewed who did not acknowledge the role their teammates played in their own rise to excellence. Football is a team game where the coordinated interplay among defensive or offensive teammates is the only way to achieve success.

"As a middle linebacker, I am only as good as my front," maintains Alondra Johnson. "If the line is getting up field and getting penetration, it makes my job a lot easier. The blocks don't get to me as quickly, and when the offensive blocking patterns are disrupted it makes my job a lot easier."

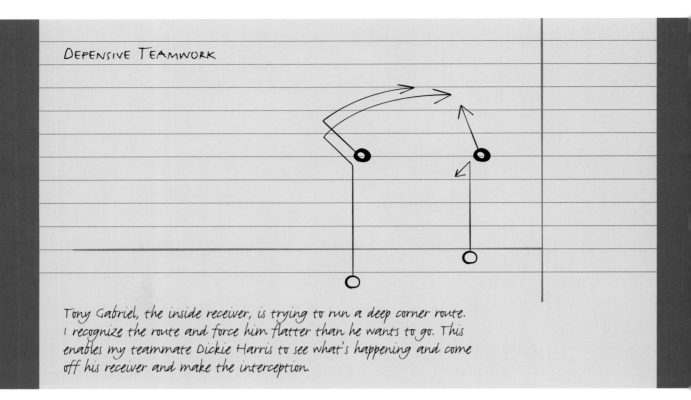

DEFENSIVE TEAMWORK

Tony Gabriel, the inside receiver, is trying to run a deep corner route. I recognize the route and force him flatter than he wants to go. This enables my teammate Dickie Harris to see what's happening and come off his receiver and make the interception.

His comments are echoed by Barron Miles, who says, "On defence, you certainly can't do it alone, especially as a defensive back. Look at Don [Matthews'] defence: if the rush does not get to the quarterback in two and a half seconds, the defensive back has almost no chance of defending against a receiver. Don likes to send everybody [to blitz six, seven or even eight players] and when the offensive timing is disrupted, it is fun to play defensive back. But when the rush doesn't get there on time, we have a desperate time out there. The CFL field is huge — the receivers can get a running start, and there is lots of interference, all of which can make for a frustrating night. Remember the 2003 Grey Cup? Edmonton had us scouted very well and found ways to buy their offence an extra second. They isolated their talented wide receivers — Ed Hervey and then Jason Tucker — on our cornerbacks and made enough big plays on offence to win the Cup."

"The players on our team have to believe in the success of the unit before their own goals," says

Matthews. He credits the fact that his defences in Montreal have consistently been at the forefront of quarterback sack totals to the whole unit, including, for example, players like Ed Philion and Robert Brown. Both, he says, were great individual pass-rushers whose sacks totals were not that high. Their teammates were getting the sacks, in part because Philion and Brown did their job. "They are playing the role asked of them," Matthews points out, "and I am happy to report they are doing it unselfishly, game in and game out. They are great for this type of defence because they take their pride in the success of the defence."

THE ULTIMATE GOAL

I played beside Hall of Fame defensive back Dickie Harris for eight years with the Alouettes. He is one of the reasons I had a long career in the CFL. He played left cornerback and I played left defensive halfback. Together with left-side linebacker Chuck Zapiec, we came to understand each other's strengths and

FROM LEFT TO RIGHT Luke Fritz, Scott Flory, Bryan Chiu, Paul Lambert and Uzooma Okeke. Okeke, Chiu and Flory have each been chosen as the CFL's Most Outstanding Lineman. Pass-rushing against these mountains of muscle can't be easy.

A WEIGHTY GAME

As Canadian football changes more and more into a passing game, so do the players change — in some cases quite dramatically. A comparison of the average weight of players in different positions shows that offensive linemen have grown significantly heavier, while entire defensive teams, no less significantly, have grown lighter.

The average weight of all the starting offensive linemen in 1990 was 268 pounds. In 2004 it was 311 pounds — a whopping forty-three-pound average increase. I assume very big men are harder to pass-rush against. Conversely, on defence the average player's weight has dropped from 228 pounds in 1990 to a slim 218 in 2004. This ten-pound decrease reflects the need for greater speed and agility in covering pass-receivers.

weaknesses and to make subtle adjustments to complex situations. We were like brothers. We could finish off one another's sentences. We instinctively knew things about each other in game situations. I came to trust Harris implicitly on the football field, and he trusted me. We often backed each other up, either trading or sharing responsibilities, and sometimes our reactions were almost the precise opposite of what the defensive playbook called for.

Harris made an interception in the Eastern final against Ottawa in 1977. He left his man in a calculated move and snatched the ball away from Ottawa's Tony Gabriel — whom I was covering at the time. We had discussed this route before the game, and I told Harris that if I noticed it developing, I would funnel Gabriel outside toward his area. Harris read the pattern like a book, and I knew, as the play was developing, that he would be there to make the play. (See diagram, opposite.)

Barron Miles discusses the importance of non-verbal communication on the field. He and linebacker Stefan Reid worked together closely over the years and achieved an effective game rapport. "We both knew what the other team's tendencies were and how the other would react to the way a play unfolded," Miles says. "Through things like film study and talk in practice, you both prepare for the same things. It can be exciting. That is a level of play you can develop if your teammates are all on the same page."

RUNNING GAME?
WHAT RUNNING GAME?

The CFL game is evolving. The passing game continues to expand in all its dimensions. Total rushing numbers are down, and passing numbers are up. Total net passing yards in a recent four-year span show an increase every year:

Year	Passing yards	Rushing yards
2002	40,542	18,953
2003	42,726	17,835
2004	46,155	16,346
2005	46,468	15,897

Me, in my early days with the Montreal Alouettes.

Wally Buono, alone with his thoughts, walks across the Frank Clair Stadium field in Ottawa during a practice two days before his Lions contest the Argonauts for the 2004 Grey Cup.

Canadian football continues to be a fascinating game. It is a game that is constantly evolving, with so many different facets that it seems at times almost impossible to analyze. The rules, the style of play and even the philosophy of the coaches continue to change. The players seem to get bigger and more athletic as time goes on, and they are required to absorb more and more information in preparing for games. Still, in the course of talking to players for this book, I have been reassured that many of what I feel are the most important aspects of the game are solidly in place. The passion, commitment and determination to succeed that were critical when I played are still in evidence today. The importance of continuous learning and the reliance on your teamates, building bonds that will last a lifetime, are as important today as they were when I stumbled about on the field. It has been a thoroughly fulfilling experience for me to talk to players who love this game. It is clear to this writer that the pursuit of excellence is alive and well in the CFL.

8

PLAYER PROFILES

DAMON ALLEN

Quarterback 6' 0", 170 lbs
Born July 29, 1973, San Diego, California
IMPORT

CFL Experience: Edmonton 1985-88,
1993-94; Ottawa 1989-91; Hamilton 1992;
Memphis 1995; B.C. 1996-2002;
Toronto 2003-

Accomplishments: CFL all-star 2005. All-time CFL records for most pass attempts, pass completions and passing yards. Third place all-time CFL rushing yards. Grey Cup wins 1987, 1993, 2000, 2004. Cup MVP 1987, 1993, 2004

Allen has passed for 69,322 yards, second to only Warren Moon for all-time pro football passing leader. The word "veteran" does not do justice to this venerable player. He is an amazing, inspirational example for all aging athletes who believe in themselves and their capacity to be productive.

BRUCE BEATON

Offensive Lineman 6' 5", 288 lbs
Born June 13, 1968, Port Hood,
Nova Scotia **CANADIAN**

CFL Experience: Edmonton 1991,
1998-2003, 2005; Ottawa 1993-94;
Calgary 1995; Montreal 1996-97

Accomplishments: CFL all-star 2000, 2001, 2003. Grey Cup wins 2003, 2005

Beaton has played in four Grey Cups. One of the acknowledged leaders of the team, both in the clubhouse and on the field, Beaton did not hesitate to let younger players know when they were not pulling their weight. During the 2005 season he sensed they were destined to win the Cup and made sure all players kept the final prize in sight.

TERRY BAKER

Kicker 6' 1", 215 lbs
Born May 8, 1962, Bridgewater,
Nova Scotia **CANADIAN**

CFL Experience: Saskatchewan
1987-89; Ottawa 1990-95; Toronto 1995;
Montreal 1996-2002

Accomplishments: CFL all-star 2001; Eastern all-star 1996 and 2001. Led CFL in scoring 1998, 2000, 2001. Grey Cup win 2002

Baker was able to finish his career the way any professional player would love to, by winning the 2002 Grey Cup.

LESS BROWNE

Defensive Back / Defensive Coach
6' 0", 185 lbs
Born December 7, 1959, East Liverpool,
Ohio **IMPORT**

CFL Experience: Hamilton 1984-86;
Winnipeg 1987-91, coach 2000-04;
Ottawa 1992; B.C. 1993-94

Accomplishments: CFL all-star 1985, 1986, 1990, 1991, 1992, 1994. CFL Hall of Fame 2002

Browne holds the CFL all-time interception record of 86 – a record made more amazing by the fact that the runner-up, Larry Highbaugh, played two more years than Browne and has only 66 interceptions. Browne is also number two on the all-time league list of blocked kicks, with 8. Browne played with a cocky, in-your-face attitude, challenging both receivers and quarterbacks – a showdown that he did not lose very often. He remains one of the most respected and feared defensive backs ever to have played in the CFL.

WALLY BUONO
Linebacker / Head Coach / General Manager 5' 10", 220 lbs
Born February 7, 1950, Potenza, Italy
CANADIAN

CFL Experience: Montreal 1972-80, coach 1983-86; Calgary coach 1987-89, head coach 1990-2002; B.C. head coach, general manager 2003-

Accomplishments: Grey Cup wins 1974, 1977. Grey Cup wins as coach 1992, 1998, 2001. CFL Coach of the Year 1992, 1993

I played with Wally Buono in Montreal for eight years, and it was evident that he was destined to be a coach. In every defensive huddle he would try to convince the defensive captain to call the defensive play he believed was the correct one. Stubborn to a fault, he has gone on to show me — and thousands of other football fanatics — that he really did know what he was talking about all those years ago.

ANTHONY CALVILLO
Quarterback 6' 2", 185 lbs
Born August 23, 1972, Los Angeles, California **IMPORT**

CFL Experience: Las Vegas 1994; Hamilton 1995-97; Montreal 1998-

Accomplishments: CFL all-star 2002, 2003; Eastern all-star 2000, 2001. CFL Most Outstanding Player 2004. Grey Cup Most Valuable Player 2002

Calvillo has thrown for more than 5,000 yards each year from 2001 to 2005, including a league-leading 6,041 yards in 2004. He is the main reason Montreal has played in four out of six Grey Cups from 2000-05.

BEN CAHOON
Wide Receiver 5' 9", 185 lbs
Born July 16, 1972, Orem, Utah
CANADIAN

CFL Experience: Montreal 1998-

Accomplishments: CFL all-star 1999, 2004, 2005; Eastern all-star 1999, 2000, 2002, 2003, 2004, 2005. CFL Most Outstanding Canadian 2002, 2003. Grey Cup win 2002

Cahoon is one of the most complete players in the entire league; a player most coaches would choose to build their team around.

HUGH CAMPBELL
Receiver / Head Coach / General Manager / President 6' 1", 180 lbs
Born May 21, 1941, Spokane, Washington
IMPORT

CFL Experience: Saskatchewan 1963-67, 1969; Edmonton head coach 1977-82, general manager 1987-97, president 1998-

Accomplishments: Grey Cup win 1966. Grey Cup wins as coach 1978, 1979, 1980, 1981, 1982. Has also coached Los Angeles (United States Football League), Houston (NFL)

A receiver known as "Gluey Huey," Campbell brought science to bear on his specialty by writing a Master's thesis on "The Catching of a Football." Ron Lancaster, Campbell's quarterback with Saskatchewan says, "Hugh was one of those players who took the game very seriously. He would stay out and run routes for as long as any quarterback would throw him footballs." As head coach of the Eskimos, he holds the best winning percentage of any CFL coach at .773.

BRYAN CHIU
Offensive Lineman 6' 2", 290 lbs
Born August 16, 1974, Vancouver,
British Columbia **CANADIAN**

CFL Experience: Montreal 1997–

Accomplishments: CFL all-star 2000, 2001, 2002, 2003, 2004, 2005.
Most Outstanding Offensive Lineman 2002

Chiu has developed into one of the most consistently excellent
offensive linemen in the league. Since his move to the centre
position in 2000, he has been a fixture on the league all-star team.
Considered one of the nastiest players in the league, he is a totally
focused competitor.

MARVIN COLEMAN
Defensive Back 5' 9", 170 lbs
Born January 31, 1972, Ocala, Florida
IMPORT

CFL Experience: Calgary 1994-2000;
Winnipeg 2001-03

Accomplishments: CFL all-star 1996, 1997, 2000. Led CFL in punt
returns 2000; led in kickoff-return yards 1997

Coleman was as accomplished a kick returner as he was a defensive
back. He holds the Calgary record for punt-return and kickoff-return
yards. One of the smartest and savviest defensive backs around, he
was able to make the players around him better.

MICHAEL "PINBALL" CLEMONS
Running Back / Slotback / Head Coach
5' 6", 170 lbs
Born January 15, 1965, Tampa Bay,
Florida **IMPORT**

CFL Experience: Toronto 1989-2000,
player/head coach 2000, head coach
2002–

Accomplishments: All-time CFL record for all-purpose yards with
25,396. Grey Cup wins 1996, 1997. Grey Cup win as head coach 2004

Clemons' infectious personality and positive outlook have made
a world of difference to the Argonauts franchise, both on and off
the football field. He is a tireless worker and wise beyond his years
– two characteristics that have allowed him to make the transition
from star receiver/running back directly to head coach. This amazing
transformation is all the more impressive because the Argos
captured the Grey Cup in only Clemons' third season as the boss.

DAVE DICKENSON
Quarterback 5' 11", 190 lbs
Born January 11, 1973, Great Falls,
Montana **IMPORT**

CFL Experience: Calgary 1995-2000;
B.C. 2003–

Accomplishments: CFL Most Outstanding Player 2000;
CFL all-star 2000

Dickenson holds the CFL record for quarterback efficiency, with the
three all-time best ratings of 118 in 2005, 114.1 in 2002 and 112.7 in
2003. He has shown an uncanny ability to generate big offensive
numbers while minimizing mistakes such as interceptions
and fumbles.

RON ESTAY
Defensive Lineman / Coach
6' 0'', 250 lbs
Born: December 22, 1948, Raceland,
Louisiana **IMPORT**

CFL Experience: Edmonton 1973-82;
Saskatchewan coach 2001-

Accomplishments: CFL all-star 1977, 1980. Western all-star 1973, 1977, 1978, 1980. Grey Cup wins 1975, 1978, 1979, 1980, 1981, 1982. CFL Hall of Fame 2003

Currently a defensive coach with the Saskatchewan Roughriders, Estay relies on the lessons he learned while playing for the dynastic Eskimos of the seventies. "I learned what type of players were needed, what type of commitment was needed and, most importantly, what type of heart was needed to be successful."

DARREN FLUTIE
Wide Receiver 5' 10'', 180 lbs
Born November 18, 1966, Manchester,
Maryland **IMPORT**

CFL Experience: B.C. 1991-95; Edmonton
1996-97; Hamilton 1998-2002

Accomplishments: CFL all-star 1996, 1997, 1999. All-time CFL pass receptions record of 972; second in all-time pass-receiving yards with 14,359

Flutie teamed up with Danny McManus for the last seven years of his illustrious career and became McManus's most reliable receiver. He was responsible for key catches in important situations, including the 1999 Grey Cup victory for Hamilton.

JOE FLEMING
Defensive Lineman 6' 3'', 285 lbs
Born: Dec. 5, 1971, Wellseley,
Massachusetts **IMPORT**

CFL Experience: B.C. 1996-97; Winnipeg
1998-99, 2004-; Calgary 2000-04

Accomplishments: CFL all-star 1998, 2000, 2001, 2003. CFL Most Outstanding Defensive Player 2003

Fleming is a wily, unselfish and experienced defensive lineman, a player teammates love to play with. He makes everyone around him better because of his knowledge and understanding of the game. A fierce competitor who asks for and gives no quarter, he is a pleasure for knowledgeable fans to watch.

DOUG FLUTIE
Quarterback 5' 10'', 175 lbs
Born October 23, 1962, Baltimore,
Maryland **IMPORT**

CFL Experience: B.C. 1990-91; Calgary
1992-95; Toronto 1995-97

Accomplishments: CFL Most Outstanding Player, 1991, 1992, 1993, 1994, 1996, 1997

With six Most Outstanding Player awards in eight years, it easy to see why many knowledgeable observers consider Flutie the greatest CFL player ever. His uncanny ability to improvise on offence enabled him to take advantage of the wide-open spaces on the CFL field, orchestrating Grey Cup victories in both Calgary and Toronto.

GENE GAINES

Defensive Back / Coach 6' 1", 180 lbs
Born June 26, 1938, Los Angeles,
California **CANADIAN**

CFL Experience: Montreal 1961,
player/coach 1970-76, coach 1977-81,
coach 1996-99; Ottawa 1962-69;
Edmonton coach 1982; Winnipeg coach
1986-90, coach 2002-03; B.C. coach 1991-94

Accomplishments: CFL Hall of Fame 1994

Altogether, Gaines spent sixteen years as a player, an amazing feat considering he played as a defensive back and kick-returner. He was my first defensive coach in 1971, a role he kept until I was traded to B.C. Lions in 1980. He continued to work as a coach continuously until his retirement in 2003, a total of 42 years of playing and coaching at the professional level.

ROB HITCHCOCK

Defensive Back 6' 1", 210 lbs
Born October 28, 1970, Hamilton,
Ontario **CANADIAN**

CFL Experience: Hamilton 1995–

Accomplishments: CFL all-star 1999, 2001, 2002. Grey Cup win 1999

Hitchcock is one of the most respected defensive backs in the league. He patrols the middle of the Tiger-Cats' secondary, stalking unsuspecting receivers and running backs, biding his time, waiting to pounce for the knockout blow. His style is "old school" in that he plays defence with a nasty disposition, constantly challenging offensive players.

ANDREW GREENE

Offensive Lineman 6' 3", 315 lbs
Born September 24, 1969, Kingston,
Jamaica **CANADIAN**

CFL Experience: Saskatchewan 1997,
1999–

Accomplishments: CFL all-star 2000, 2003, 2004, 2005. CFL Most Outstanding Offensive Lineman 2003

Greene is the epitome of the strong, silent type – an archetypal offensive lineman. No one has an easy game against him. He is equally adept as a run-blocker or pass-blocker.

ALONDRA JOHNSON

Linebacker 5' 11", 200 lbs
Born July 22, 1965, Gardena, California
IMPORT

CFL Experience: B.C. 1989–90; Calgary
1991-2003

Accomplishments: CFL all-star 1995, 1998, 2000; Western all-star 1991, 1992, 1997, 1998, 2000. Second in all-time defensive tackles with 1,084. Grey Cup wins 1992, 1998, 2001

Johnson is one of the fiercest, most determined defensive players ever to put on a uniform – a team leader in every sense of the word.

RON LANCASTER

Quarterback / Head Coach / General Manager 5' 10", 190 lbs
Born October 14, 1938, Fairchance, Pennsylvania **CANADIAN**

CFL Experience: Ottawa 1960-62; Saskatchewan 1963-1978, head coach 1978-80; Edmonton head coach 1991-97; Hamilton head coach 1998-2003, general manager 2004

Accomplishments: CFL all-star 1970, 1973, 1975, 1976. CFL Most Outstanding Player 1970, 1976. CFL Hall of Fame 1982

Lancaster led Saskatchewan during their glory years of the 1960s and 1970s. He has continued to work in the CFL in a multitude of ways, including a stint as a television commentator. He is currently the Tiger-Cats' senior director of football operations and can be called upon to provide a lifelong perspective on the Canadian game.

GENE MAKOWSKY

Offensive Lineman 6' 3", 300 lbs
Born April 17, 1973, Saskatoon, Saskatchewan **CANADIAN**

CFL Experience: Saskatchewan 1995-

Accomplishments: CFL all-star 2004, 2005. CFL Most Outstanding Offensive Lineman 2004, 2005

Makowsky has played his entire career with the "Green Riders," a dream come true for a local boy. The dream has gotten better the longer he plays. Makowsky is widely regarded as one of the finest all-round offensive lineman currently playing in the CFL, the anchor of what is arguably the best offensive line in the league.

MARV LEVY

Head Coach
Born August 3, 1928, Chicago, Illinois
IMPORT

CFL Experience: Montreal head coach 1973-77

Accomplishments: Grey Cup wins 1975, 1977. Has also coached Kansas City (NFL), Buffalo (NFL)

Levy brought a high level of professionalism to the Montreal Alouettes organization when he arrived in 1973. His insistence that players become accountable both to themselves and their teammates laid the foundation for the Als' amazing run of five Grey Cup appearances from 1974-79. Levy took his approach to both life and football south of the border, where he coached the Buffalo Bills to four consecutive Super Bowl appearances.

GREG MARSHALL

Defensive Lineman / Coach
6' 3", 255 lbs
Born Beverly, Maryland **IMPORT**

CFL Experience: Ottawa 1980-88, defensive coordinator 2005- ; Saskatchewan coach 1997-2002; Edmonton defensive coordinator 2003-04

Accomplishments: CFL Most Oustanding Defensive Player 1983. CFL all-star 1981, 1983

Marshall was known as a complete defensive lineman, equally proficient at stopping the run and as a pass-rusher.

DON MATTHEWS

Head Coach
Born June 22, 1939, Amesbury,
Massachusetts **CANADIAN**

CFL Experience: Edmonton coach
1977-82, head coach 1999-2000; B.C.
head coach 1983-87; Baltimore head
coach 1994-95; Toronto head coach
1990, 1996-97; Saskatchewan head coach 1991-93; Montreal head
coach 2002-

Accomplishments: Grey Cup wins as head coach 1985, 1995, 1996,
1997, 2002. All-time CFL record for regular-season wins as coach

Matthews is the CFL's longest-serving head coach. In four years
as the Alouette head coach, he took the team to three Grey Cups,
capturing the trophy in 2002 – his first year on the job. He is a defensive
specialist with a penchant for gambling, using attacking defensive game
plans, a philosophy he has employed with great success.

BARRON MILES

Defensive Back 5' 9'', 180 lbs
Born January 1, 1972, Roselle,
New Jersey **IMPORT**

CFL Experience: Montreal 1998-2004;
B.C. 2005-

Accomplishments: CFL all-star 1999, 2000, 2002. CFL Rookie of
the Year 1998. Grey Cup win 2002

Miles is the number two all-time kick blocker with eight blocks.
He can play any of the defensive-back positions with style and class.
He is known more for his finesse than ferocity. He is the type of
defensive back that a coach would love to build his scheme around,
using Miles' brains and insight to develop the secondary.

DANNY MCMANUS

Quarterback 6' 0'', 200 lbs
Born June 17, 1965, Dania, Florida
IMPORT

CFL Experience: Winnipeg 1990-92; B.C.
1993-95; Edmonton 1996-97, 2006- ;
Hamilton 1998-2005

Accomplishments: CFL all-star 1999. Grey Cup win and Cup MVP 1999

McManus has thrown for more than 53,000 yards, number two all-
time behind Damon Allen. He will never be considered a scrambler,
rather he is known for his quick release and his almost stoic manner
as the on-field general. Remarkably, he has found ways to remain
competitive past his fortieth birthday.

DERRELL "MOOKIE" MITCHELL

Slot Back 5' 8'', 190 lbs
Born September 16, 1971, Miami, Florida
IMPORT

CFL Experience: Toronto 1997-2004;
Edmonton 2005-

Accomplishments: CFL all-star 1997, 1998, 2000. All-time CFL record
for catches in one season with 160. CFL Rookie of the Year 1997. Grey
Cup wins 1997, 2004, 2005

In nine seasons Mitchell has accumulated over 10,700 receiving
yards, a feat only seven other receivers can match. Mitchell found a
new home in Edmonton in 2005, contributing 94 receptions for 1,207
yards, a major factor in the team's Grey Cup victory.

JOE MONTFORD

Defensive End 6' 1'', 225 lbs
Born July 30, 1970, Columbia, South
Carolina **IMPORT**

CFL Experience: Shreveport 1995;
Hamilton 1996-2001, 2003-04; Toronto
2002; Edmonton 2005-

Accomplishments: CFL all-star 1998, 1999, 2000, 2001, 2002. CFL Most
Outstanding Defensive Player 1998, 2000, 2001. Grey Cup wins 1999, 2005

To most keen observers, Montford has been, the premier rush end in
the league since 1996 – a man who gives nervous feet to the
offensive tackles lined up across from him on the line of scrimmage.
His speed, quickness and savvy make him a handful for any player,
and his quarterback sack total of 134 (fifth all-time in the CFL), and
defensive tackle total of 532 (tenth all-time), testify to his uncanny
ability to play great defence.

MIKE O'SHEA

Linebacker 6' 3'', 225 lbs
Born September 21, 1970, North Bay,
Ontario **CANADIAN**

CFL Experience: Hamilton 1993-95,
2000; Toronto 1996-99, 2001-

Accomplishments: CFL all-star 1999; Eastern all-star 1994, 1995, 1997,
1999, 2000. CFL Most Outstanding Rookie 1993. Grey Cup wins 1996,
1997, 2004

O'Shea has been the epitome of the CFL middle linebacker, the
cornerstone of the Argonauts defensive team, making defensive
calls, adjustments and exceptional plays. He ranks number three in
all-time defensive tackles with 968, behind only Alondra Johnson
and Willie Pless.

TRAVIS MOORE

Slotback 6' 1'', 193 lbs
Born August 5, 1970, Santa Monica,
California **IMPORT**

CFL Experience: Calgary 1994-2002;
Saskatchewan 2003-

Accomplishments: CFL all-star 1999, 2000, 2001. Gery Cup wins
1998, 2001

Moore has been a model of consistency, gaining a total of 9,930
receiving yards, enough to rank him tenth among the great CFL
receivers.

UZOOMA OKEKE

Offensive Tackle 6' 0'', 310 lbs
Born September, 3 1970, Beaumont,
Texas **IMPORT**

CFL Experience: Shreveport 1994-95;
Ottawa 1996; Montreal 1997-

Accomplishments: CFL all-star 1997, 1998, 1999, 2002, 2003, 2004,
2005. CFL Most Outstanding Lineman 1999; runner-up 1998, 2004.
Grey Cup win 2002

Okeke is recognized by his peers as the best offensive lineman in the
CFL, as well as the best pass-blocker. This quiet, unassuming chunk
of granite has been the anchor of the Alouettes' offensive line since
his arrival in Montreal.

PAUL OSBALDISTON

Punter / Kicker 6' 3", 210 lbs
Born April, 27, 1964, Oldham, England
CANADIAN

CFL Experience: B.C., Winnipeg,
Hamilton 1986; Hamilton 1986-2003

Accomplishments: CFL all-star 1996, 1998, 2001. Eastern all-star 1998, 1990, 1996, 1998, 2000, 2001. Grey Cup wins 1986, 1999

For seventeen of his eighteen seasons in the CFL, Osbaldiston handled all the kicking duties for the Hamilton Tiger-Cats, amassing an amazing total of 2,339 points, second only to the unmatchable Lui Passaglia. Osbaldiston has also totalled 63 points in Grey Cup games, second only to Edmonton's Dave Cutler.

ELFRID PAYTON

Defensive End 6' 1", 230 lbs
Born September, 22, 1967, Gretna,
Louisiana **IMPORT**

CFL Experience: Winnipeg 1991-93,
2000; Shreveport 1994; Baltimore
1994-95; Montreal 1996-99; Toronto
2001; Edmonton 2002-04

Accomplishments: CFL all-star 1993, 1997, 1998, 2001. CFL Most Outstanding Defensive Player 2002. Grey Cup wins 1995, 2003

Payton was, in his own words, a specialist. He ended his career with 154 quarterback sacks, second only to Grover Covington for the CFL lead. He was an enigma to some, frustrating coaches with his unorthodox and undisciplined style of play, but he produced results wherever he went. He participated in Grey Cup finals in 1993, 1994, 1995, 2002 and 2003.

LUI PASSAGLIA

Kicker / Punter 5' 10", 190 lbs
Born June 7, 1954, Vancouver,
British Columbia **CANADIAN**

CFL Experience: B.C. 1978-2002;

Accomplishments: Holds most all-time CFL kicking records, including most points, most field goals, and most punt and kickoff yards. Grey Cup wins 1985, 1994, 2000

What more can be said about a player who was in the game for twenty-five consecutive years and set a string of records that may never be broken? I played with him as a member of the Lions and came to know him as an extremely knowledgeable, competitive player and as a strong, caring personality. He is currently responsible for community relations with the Lions organization, a job for which he is perfectly suited.

ALLEN PITTS

Receiver 6' 4", 200 lbs
Born June 28, 1963, Tucson, Arizona
IMPORT

CFL Experience: Calgary 1990-2000

Accomplishments: CFL all-star 1991, 1992, 1994, 1995, 1998, 1999. Holds CFL record for receiving yards with 14,891. Grey Cup wins 1994, 1998

Pitts is often considered the best receiver ever to play in the CFL. He combined a strong work ethic, leadership and knowledge of the game with exceptional athletic skills. Dave Dickenson has said that Pitts ran the most beautifully crafted pass routes and had an amazing ability to come up with a big catch at key moments in a game.

MIKE PRINGLE

Running Back 5' 8", 190 lbs
Born October 1, 1997, Los Angeles,
California **IMPORT**

CFL Experience: Edmonton 1992,
2003-04; Sacramento 1993; Baltimore
1994-95; Montreal 1996-2002

Accomplishments: CFL all-star 1994, 1995, 1997, 1998, 1999, 2000, 2003. CFL Most Outstanding Player 1997, 1999. Grey Cup wins 1995, 2002, 2003

Pringle holds most CFL all-time rushing records, including most rushing yards with 16,425. One of the most focused, determined players ever to suit up, he played with an amazing singularity of purpose. He was truly an inspiration, to players and fans alike.

GEROY SIMON

Receiver 6' 0", 190 lbs
Born September 11, 1975, Johnstown,
Pennsylvania **IMPORT**

CFL Experience: Winnipeg 1999-2000;
B.C. 2001-

Accomplishments: CFL all-star 2003, 2004

From 2002 to 2005, coinciding with the Lions' acquisition of Dave Dickenson as quarterback, Simon emerged as one of the main receiving threats in the league. He caught no fewer than 94 passes in each of those three years and led in receiving yards in 2004.

STEFEN REID

Linebacker 6' 2", 220 lbs
Born May 11, 1972, Merritt,
British Columbia **CANADIAN**

CFL Experience: Ottawa 1995; Montreal
1996-2002

Accomplishments: Eastern all-star 2002. Grey Cup win 2002

Reid has not compiled the outstanding statistics of most other players selected for this book, but in the five years I knew him as a member of the Alouettes I came to respect his vast knowledge and his fascination with the game. He is an example of the type of player who has perhaps limited athletic prowess, but who can thrive in this game by finding a role and playing smart. There was no more important player on the Montreal defence when the Alouettes defeated the Edmonton Eskimos in the 2002 Grey Cup final.

MILT STEGALL

Slotback 6' 0", 185 lbs
Born January 25, 1970, Cincinnati, Ohio
IMPORT

CFL Experience: Winnipeg 1995-

Accomplishments: CFL Most Outstanding Player 2002;
CFL all-star 1997, 2000, 2001, 2002

Stegall is a touchdown-producing machine. From 1995 through 2005, he caught passes across the goal line 126 times, 9 more than the amazing Allen Pitts and 26 more times than the next closest receiver. He holds the CFL record for highest average gain per pass at an astounding 26.5 yards. In addition, he has accumulated 12,318 receiving yards to rank sixth all-time among CFL receivers.

JAMIE TARAS

Offensive Lineman 6' 2", 280 lbs
Born January 31, 1966, Acton, Ontario
CANADIAN

CFL Experience: B.C. 1987-2002

Accomplishments: CFL all-star 1995, 1999. Western all-star 1999, 2000, 2002. Most Outstanding Lineman 1999. Grey Cup wins 1994, 2000

Taras made the interesting transition from running back to offensive lineman and used his athletic ability and knowledge of the game to thrive in the league for fifteen productive years. He played with his heart and his head, demonstrating leadership on and off the field.

TERRY VAUGHN

Receiver 5' 9", 205 lbs
Born December 25, 1971, Sumter,
South Carolina **IMPORT**

CFL Experience: Calgary 1995-98;
Edmonton 1999-2004; Montreal 2005-

Accomplishments: CFL all-star 1998, 2001, 2002, 2003. Grey Cup wins 1998, 2003

With 13,051 receiving yards and 948 receptions, Vaughn continues to march toward Allen Pitts' and Darren Flutie's records as the CFL leaders in these categories. His most startling statistic, however – of which he is probably the proudest – is the minimum of 1,000 yards he has gained in each of his seasons in the league. He is focused, determined, conditioned, mentally tough and competitive. He is the ideal model for a CFL receiver and one of the truly great players in the league.

GERALD VAUGHN

Defensive Back / Linebacker
6' 3", 205 lbs
Born April 8, 1970, Abbeville,
Mississippi **IMPORT**

CFL Experience: Calgary 1993-95;
Winnipeg 1996; Hamilton 1997-2001;
Ottawa 2003-

Accomplishments: CFL all-star 1998, 1999. Grey Cup win 1999

Vaughn is unquestionably one of the toughest defensive players active in the CFL today. Receivers hate to face him – his long arms and mean disposition make for a long night on the field. He holds the all-time CFL record of 12 blocked kicks.

PIERRE VERCHEVAL

Offensive Lineman 6' 1", 275 lbs
Born November 22, 1964, Quebec City,
Quebec **CANADIAN**

CFL Experience: Edmonton 1988-92;
Toronto 1993-97; Montreal 1998-2001

Accomplishments: CFL all-star 1992, 1994, 1997, 1998, 1999, 2000. Most Outstanding Offensive Lineman 2000. Grey Cup wins 1996, 1997

Vercheval played a total of 212 regular season games, thirteen playoff games and four Grey Cup games. Like most offensive linemen, Vercheval became better with age, and he was a foundation of the Alouettes line that shepherded Mike Pringle through his glory years – including the 1998 season where Pringle gained 2,065 yards. He is now considered one of the most knowledgeable football analysts in the country, working in the French-language media in Quebec.

Picture Credits

Puzant Apkarian with Ed Homonylo: Front cover.

© **Shaun Best/Reuters/Corbis:** Back cover (bottom), 156-157.

© **Bettmann/Corbis:** 27, 32-33.

Canadian Press: Back cover (top right), 6-7, 10, 21 (bottom left), 25, 28-29, 39, 41, 44, 44-45, 45, 60-61, 71, 76, 77, 78-79, 98, 99, 118-119, 136, 136-137, 142-143, 146-147, 148, 148-149, 149, 155, 158-159, 166-167, 177, 179 (top right, bottom left), 180 (except top right), 181 (bottom right), 182, 183 (except top left), 184 (top right, bottom left), 185, 186 (bottom left, bottom right), 187 (except top right), 188 (top left, bottom left), 189 (top right).

Bryan Chiu: 51.

Kyle Clapham: 2, 36 (sidebar), 67 (sidebar), 94-95, 100 (sidebar), 106, 110-111, 126.

Corephoto.ca: 13 (sidebar), 19, 30-31, 92-93, 150-151, 181 (bottom left).

Pablo Galvez/www.CanProPhoto.com: 43 (sidebar), 99 (sidebar), 108 (sidebar), 114 (sidebar), 149 (sidebar), 170-171, 176 (sidebar), 178.

© **Jeff Goode/Toronto Star/First Light:** 32.

F. Scott Grant: Back cover (top left), 18, 23, 24, 26, 52-53, 54-55, 57 (sidebar), 59, 63, 68, 82 (sidebar), 85 (bottom), 102-103, 109, 123 (sidebar), 127, 154, 160-161.

Ted Grant: 96.

Derrell Mitchell: 35.

Benoit Pelosse: 10-11, 12-13, 56, 64-65, 73, 104, 110.

Tony Proudfoot: 8-9, 113, 176.

© **Reuters/Corbis:** 138.

John Sokolowski: 4-5, 14-15, 16-17, 17, 21 (except bottom left), 34-35, 37, 38, 42, 43, 48 (sidebar), 49, 50, 54, 66, 73 (sidebar), 74-75, 81, 82, 85 (top), 86, 88, 89, 91, 107 (sidebar), 115, 116, 119, 120, 120-121, 121, 122, 128, 131, 132-133, 134, 141, 144, 144-145, 152-153, 163, 164, 168, 173, 175 (including sidebar), 179 (top left, bottom right), 180 (top right), 181 (top left, top right), 183 (top left), 184 (top left, bottom right), 186 (top left, top right), 187 (top right), 188 (top right, bottom right), 189 (except top right).

Acknowledgments

I would like to thank the dozens of current and former CFL players, coaches and office staff who have been both gracious and patient, allowing me to explore, in depth, their connection to this great game.

It took considerable effort for me to put into words what I have long held to be important factors in one's ability to play football at this level. There are many people who deserve thanks for their part in assisting me in this process. The greatest influence came from Dr. Ted Wall, my old high school football coach, Master's advisor and longtime friend. He provided the right level of encouragement, edited my words, gave suggestions and showed much patience in getting me over my insecurities and into high gear with the manuscript.

Thanks to Dick Irvin for helping me locate Chris Jackson of Madison Press Books, who was the first to see promise in my idea for this book. Thanks also to the rest of the crew at Madison, including Oliver Salzmann and Imoinda Romain, and to Jonathan Webb, Jim Hynes and others who worked to get my ideas into such a beautiful format.

A host of others need mentioning as well, for providing timely assistance to this stumbling, first-time author, including all nine CFL teams' communications staff, photographers and media personnel. Special thanks to the Alouettes' Kevin Strasser, Noel Thorpe, Louis-Philippe Dorais, Noah Sidel, Colin Farquharson and Ronnie James. Thanks to my broadcasting partner Rick Moffat of CJAD in Montreal, who gave me much-needed advice on early editions of the manuscript. As well, Steve Milton of the *Hamilton Spectator* gave his honest professional opinion. Thanks also to my biggest critics and my biggest fans: my family — Vicki, my patient and understanding wife, as well as Michael, Lindsay and Lauren.

— *Tony Proudfoot*

First&Goal

was produced by

MADISON PRESS BOOKS
1000 Yonge Street, Suite 200
Toronto, Ontario, Canada
M4W 2K2
www.madisonpressbooks.com

Manuscript Editor: JONATHAN WEBB
Photo Research: JIM HYNES
Executive Editor: IMOINDA ROMAIN
Editorial Director: WANDA NOWAKOWSKA

Design: COSTA LECLERC DESIGN

Production Manager: SANDRA HALL, DONNA CHONG
Production Director: SUSAN BARRABLE

Director, Business Development: CHRISTOPHER JACKSON
Publisher: OLIVER SALZMANN